10 —

D1596123

The Tyranny of the Moderns

The Tyranny of
the Moderns

NADIA URBINATI

Translated by Martin Thom

Yale UNIVERSITY PRESS
New Haven and London

The translation of this book has been funded by SEPS—Segretariato Europeo per le Pubblicazioni Scientifiche, Via Val d'Aposa 7, 40123 Bologna, Italy. E-mail: seps@seps.it. Web site: www.seps.it.

The author expresses appreciation to the Warner Fund at the University Seminars at Columbia University for help in publication. Material in this work was presented to the University Seminar: Studies in Political and Social Thought.

Originally published as *Liberi e uguali*. Copyright © 2011 by Gius. Laterza & Figli. All rights reserved.
Published by arrangement with Marco Vigevani Agenzia Letteraria.

Yale University Press books may be purchased in quantity for educational, business, or promotional use. For information, please e-mail sales. press@yale.edu (U.S. office) or sales@yaleup.co.uk (U.K. office).

Set in Minion type by IDS Infotech Ltd., Chandigarh, India.
Printed in the United States of America.

Library of Congress Cataloging-in-Publication Data

Urbinati, Nadia, 1955–
[Liberi e uguali. English]
The tyranny of the moderns / Nadia Urbinati; translated by Martin Thom.
    pages cm
Originally published in Italian under title: Liberi e uguali
Includes bibliographical references and index.
ISBN 978-0-300-18277-4 (hardback)
1. Individualism—Political aspects. 2. Democracy. I. Title.
JC571.U7313 2015
323'.04201—dc23
                                                                    2014027079

A catalogue record for this book is available from the British Library.

This paper meets the requirements of ANSI/NISO Z39.48-1992 (Permanence of Paper).

10 9 8 7 6 5 4 3 2 1

Contents

Introduction 1

ONE Democratic Individualism 12

TWO Private Happiness 28

THREE An "Ism" to Be Used with Caution 37

FOUR A Brief History of Individualism 49

FIVE The Individual against Politics 70

SIX Economic Individualism 88

SEVEN Apathy and Solitude 109

EIGHT Identitarian Community 125

NINE Regeneration 140

TEN Judgment and Disagreement 167

Notes 187

Index 207

Introduction

The will of an entire people cannot make just what is unjust.

—Benjamin Constant, 1815

The identification of individualism with a vision of life that is reflected in the maxim "I don't give a damn" is virtually a truism. I suspect that Italy, the original inspiration for this observation, is no exception. This maxim can be read in two different ways, that is to say, either as the heedless expression of deplorable sentiments like egoism and a supreme indifference to the fate of others, or else as the plucky and all-but-heroic demeanor of persons able to laugh in the face of misfortune, to pick themselves up and to dust themselves down. Yet in this latter case, too, individualism is extolled not for its own sake but rather in the guise of certain vicarious qualities that are associated with it, such as the courage to take risks, to assume responsibility for one's own actions, and to practice self-help. Economists and political administrators who vie with one another in seeing who can cut

1

the most taxes for the well-off do not justify their plans in terms of the maxim "I don't give a damn," even if this would be a perfect description of the logic of their fiscal policy. They stress instead the individual contribution to the general well-being that de-taxing dividends would make possible, noting the natural return to society that the freeing of individuals from the fetters of social obligation would allow. They construe individualism as a kind of social concern and even as a form of generosity! The fact is that underlying the policy and ideology of the "trickle-down" effect there is the assumption that taxation is not supposed to serve, say, education or health care, because in the ideal world of a self-regulated market society these needs would be satisfied by individuals themselves, with no help from others or from "society." Receiving assistance, or so this ideology has it, is a sign that the individual has been defeated; welfare policies are, it is argued, a remedy for the failure of persons. Hence education and health care are private commodities, not conditions for the performance of individuals in a democratic society.

Thus, whereas the word "individualism" bears the stigma of negative moral sentiments like egoism or indifference to the fate of others, the hegemonic morality that individualism is associated with has been and is praised for its bold flouting of, and imperious disdain for, regulations and social responsibilities. This hegemonic morality is indeed consistent with the maxim "I don't give a damn," although ashamed to confess it openly. It argues that if each of us is individually responsible for her or his own life, as we must be if we are to deserve some return from society, we alone are to blame if things go wrong. So permeated is the social and economic organization of our Western societies (some more than others) by this individualistic ethos that it can seem grossly naïve to blame "the system" for our adversities, and, moreover, wrong even to think of using state policy to correct personal defeats. All in all, this ethos is the fulcrum of our society, the vital impulse of our moral life, and indeed the motive power behind whatever is alleged to be valuable in it: entrepreneurial restlessness, affluence, the heroic sense of one's own responsibilities, and, above all, merit as the sole legitimate precondition of reward for our efforts. "The recrudescent ideology of individualism, with its concomitant implications that the members of a society owe nothing to one another and that personal merit determines success or failure, has thus had an unopposed hearing."[1] These are the basic ingredients of the right-wing propaganda that has managed to turn into a value what in the popular culture bore (and still bears in many countries, or at any rate in specific parts of their populations) the stigma of a selfish morality.

The popular and oft-repeated reaction to the hegemonic morality of individualism has been communitarianism, which is rehearsed in several different forms, for example, as a republican ideal of patriotic devotion to one's own country and nation or as an unmediated sense of belonging unreservedly to one's "people," religious community, or ethnic group.[2] Since the 1980s, communitarianism has been the most representative critical voice raised against liberalism and its individualistic foundation, whether phrased in terms of social justice or as a neoliberal panacea.[3] In practice, communitarian philosophies did have some positive consequences, since they drew attention to the justified resistance of minority cultures to the overbearing culture of the majority, and moreover to the demand that minorities suffering discrimination be accorded recognition and equal consideration. Yet as an ideology, communitarianism is tailored to suit a nostalgic vision of certain idealized traditions that would ineluctably be swept away by the practice and culture of rights. Indeed, the communitarian response to individualism is to challenge the culture of rights. Solidarity with "our own people" and unity with those who are for some specified reasons similar to us has been perhaps the most seductive and flamboyant riposte to the vision of life expressed by the maxim "I don't give a damn." Yet in truth this nostrum does not offer a convincing alternative to the ideology of individualism. Ironically enough, communitarianism is a form of individualism applied to the group itself. (Indeed, here too the "I" is the criterion in relation to which solidarity with others is evoked, since the rationale for selecting the recipients of our solidarity is their possession of certain qualities resembling the ones "we" recognize as "ours.") Furthermore, communitarianism is entirely compatible with the devastating effects that the ideology of individualism can have, since it cultivates the moral precepts of compassion and charity, two important strategies that, while they may silence a guilty conscience, do nonetheless block any notion that society should set about eliminating the conditions of misery that solicit compassion and charity in the first place. Communitarian solidarity is intended to be an alternative to the policies of the welfare state and in this sense is an important ally of the ideology of individualism, since it too is suspicious of all attempts to replace individual moral engagement with social justice. Given its functional role in attenuating the consequences of the hegemonic morality of individualism, the communitarian identification with certain foundational values has been accorded more than its fair share of attention, at any rate so far as the critique of the maxim "I don't give a damn" is concerned. Another path is, however, open to us, one that permits a critical assessment of that selfsame ideology, and this time from the perspective not of communitarian but of political identity.

For all its extraordinary popularity, the identification of individualism with egoism does no favors to democratic society and is indeed unwarranted. Individualism as an idea associated with thinking with one's head (thus being predisposed to dissent rather than to a merging with the community), claiming an equal dignity, and enjoying an equal right to suffrage and voice is the political and ideal foundation of democracy, and should be equated neither with antisocial egoism nor with indifference toward others and toward politics. Rather than seeking for alternatives to individualism in the guise of communitarianism, this book proposes that we rescue individualism from its lethal identification with the ideology of individualism—as epitomized in the maxim "I don't give a damn"—in order to recover its political meaning. Moreover, it argues that the rescue of individualism from the ideology of individualism will serve as a defense of democratic citizenship. This renders the distinction between different forms of individualism anything but a pointless, scholastic exercise.

In the eighteenth and still more in the nineteenth and early twentieth centuries, there was forged an idea that remains valuable and appealing, namely, "transcendental individualism," a philosophical perspective according attention to the person in her or his specific and concrete circumstance, and with it an ethical language rendering possible coordination of competences and respect for differences. Attention to the individual person and to her or his capacity to cooperate with others as equals in rights and dignity; attention to that individual person as a free and autonomous being whose judgment is at the source of the legitimacy of political authority: these are the political characteristics of democratic individualism. It is by no means only in liberal texts that a belief in the political implications of the value ascribed to the individual person may be discerned.

I have always been struck, for example, by the words the young Antonio Gramsci used to represent this same idea: "a sense of initiative, respect for others, the conviction that liberty for all is the sole guarantee of individual liberties, that scrupulous observance of contracts is the indispensable precondition for society."[4]

Reverting to earlier political debates is by no means an anachronistic exercise. Indeed, to judge by the current predicament of Western societies mired in chronic economic crisis, attitudes and opinions do not seem to have changed overmuch compared with the mid-nineteenth century, when the term "individualism" was coined, and when the capitalist system first manifested its contradictory tendencies, with its bursts of technological innovation and economic growth being repeatedly offset by the systemic production of exploitation and misery. Albeit with the difference, which is not a trifling one, that our countries are not in the grip of political oligarchies as they were in the nineteenth century but instead are constitutional democracies made up of citizens who in the course of often bloody struggles have succeeded in winning, extending, and multiplying their rights, civil and social. Individualism, which in recent years has assumed an arrogant and vulgar guise that never ceases to amaze, is characteristic of a modern society that is structurally individualist, composed of citizens who are subject to social and political rules based upon the principle of equal freedoms and opportunities; in other words, who share the culture of rights. How can we deplore individualism if individualism is the defining feature of democracy and if by the same token we hold democracy to be a good?

Early critics of modernity like the antiegalitarian Thomas Carlyle or the republican Giuseppe Mazzini, just to name two of the most representative intellectuals of the century in which modern society acquired an individualist character and individualism attained the status of an ideology, combated individualism either in the name of a hierarchical and authoritarian society or in that of a solidaristic state sustained by citizens imbued with patriotic virtues and intent upon cultivating national identity. It is hard to conceive just what a resurrected Carlyle or Mazzini would make of life today. Disturbed by anarchy and rebellion, they proposed solutions that would restore order and political stability. As is all too plain, the resistance of civil society to the state in the name of individual interests is much as it was in the nineteenth century, except that, despite the fears of the abovementioned prophets, it does not give rise either to rebellion or to anarchy. On the contrary, impatience with regulations and red tape and with the laws of the state tends to assume the guise of an uncritical adherence to the logic of individual interest; instead of fomenting anarchy, it fosters an almost perfect identification with a model of society cast as a vast market in which anything and everything can feasibly be an object of exchange, where money, sex, and power are at one and the same time goals and prizes of private and public success, and where the language of the public good seems itself to have gone missing, the implication being that this same public good is a thing that penalizes individual merit rather than a condition for rewarding it.

An individualism of this stripe, possessive and conformist, litigious and docile, all too prone to manipulate norms and to submit to the tyrannical sway of private interests, is consonant with the image of a society lacking an array of ethical impulses functioning as a gravitational force, such as respect for others, whether fellow citizens or not; equality as the source of political autonomy; solidarity as amity between citizens but also as empathy between fellow human beings. Without such ethical impulses pertaining at once to the individual and to the citizen, the individual liberty which civil rights guarantee and exalt may face two risks: that of being taken for granted or regarded as a natural given, since to have rights also means being able to live one's own everyday existence with a modicum of safety and almost without being aware of them; and that of becoming a privilege of some rather than of others, so as to be erroneously identified with the particular rights enjoyed by those who are a majority in a given territory by virtue of voting, opinion, or tradition. In the former case, being accustomed to living in a society that guarantees liberty may lead citizens to become politically indifferent and apathetic, causing them to succumb to the illusion that the norms written into the Constitution or the Bill of Rights and the routine functioning of the institutions suffice to render their liberty safe. Rights seem able to reproduce themselves without requiring any special attention on the part of the citizens aside from their abiding by the law. In the latter case, right is sundered from the culture of respect and equality and thereby becomes the equivalent of a privilege that excludes and rejects, and so much so that it ends up losing the requisite qualities of "defense from" and "limitation upon" power, acquiring instead those of domination and the will to power, radical distortions of right because of the identification of this privilege with the power of the strongest, whether they are such by dint of being economically more powerful or through being the majority. These are two correlated forms of depoliticization, or the degrading of the role of politics through the impact on the one hand of a transformation of rights into a routine functioning of the institutions in relation to which individuals are mere recipients, and on the other hand of a predatory expansion of the mentality of possession from economic relations to political relations. This inversion of meaning, which often has effects in everyday life and administrative practice, sunders equality from liberty, as if the latter could only exist on condition that it be enjoyed not by all equally but as a privilege of some (and not others), and as if the former were identical with a given specificity or an essence, cultural or social, belonging to a specific group instead of being the name of a public relationship that is meant to treat persons who are different with equal respect and as equal political agents. The sundering of equality from liberty is the mirror image of a profound transformation in ideology and in the formation of sentiments, and one that facilitates the turning of democratic individualism into an individualism that is antisocial and tyrannical, or apathetic and indifferent toward the fate of the wider human community, whether national or universal. If the study of individualism is important, it is because through it we may apprehend and critically understand this disquieting phenomenon of a redefinition of civil liberty in terms of the logic of *ownership* (individual and/or collective), and of democracy in the light of collective ideology and the power of the majority.

Critics like Carlyle and Mazzini regarded individualism as a vice, and their critique was at once a lament and a condemnation, from which one would be hard-pressed to obtain anything other than solutions that were each as unappealing as the other, namely, on the one hand the establishment of a hierarchical order in which a person's value depended on her or his functions or social status, and on the other a pedagogic paternalism exercised by virtuous and patriotic citizens in the name of and for the good of all. These are not the paths to follow if one wishes to attempt a critical reading of the ideology of individualism that is consistent with democratic ideals and principles. The path I propose to take in this book is the one

suggested by the sociopolitical analysis of Alexis de Tocqueville
in *Democracy in America* (1835–1840). Tocqueville set out to
treat individualism as a political, not a moral, category. He
designated it as a "reflective sentiment" of citizens who live
together on the basis of democratic principles and institutions,
and also of individuals who operate in a market economy on
the basis of calculations of interest. This, I suggest, should
be the starting point for any critical analysis: a dual identity of
the political and the socioeconomic, or the citizen and the
individual. Our reassessment, and even reconstitution, of this
dual identity should help us to understand just how it is that
individualism needs to be defended from the ideology of individualism. Why is it important to set out from this political
premise? For two reasons: first of all because a clear grasp of
the character of democratic individualism enables us to subject
individualism as such to a coherent critical analysis; second, in
order to prevent the critique of individualist ideology from
veering off toward anti-individualist solutions, which, being
at odds with the idea of rights onto which constitutional democracy has been grafted, are dangerously exposed to a communitarian identification of democracy with the culture and the
political will of the overall majority. Now, if we ponder the
phenomena that loom largest in our imaginations—those
of apathy or tyrannical and possessive individualism—we see
that, although extreme, these forms are not eccentric in a con-
stitutionally based democratic society and culture. In order
to anticipate in a few brief phrases the central theme of this
book, we might say that the relationship between liberty and
equality is the thematic crux enabling us to understand and
to evaluate the meaning of individualism in democratic society,
but also to discern and to criticize its distortions and aberrations; to distinguish, in other words, between the various

different forms of individualism. The main point is to resituate individualism within the political construed as a democratic domain, wherein, as Tocqueville surmised, it first arose, and to wrest it back from the private domain of interests in which it has been held captive in recent decades. The aim of this book is thus to recover the meaning, role, and vocation of the citizen as the political subject or the fundamental agent of democratic society, an agent who is free and equal in the sense implicit in democratic procedures and principles, and in all that they promise.

I

Democratic Individualism

At that stage one can imagine a society in which all men, regarding the law as their common work, would love it and submit to it without difficulty; the authority of the government would be respected as necessary, not as sacred; the love felt toward the head of the state would not be a passion but a calm and rational feeling. Each man having some rights and being sure of the enjoyment of those rights, there would be established between all classes a manly confidence and a sort of reciprocal courtesy, as far removed from pride as from servility.

Understanding its own interests, the people would appreciate that in order to enjoy the benefits of society one must shoulder its obligations. Free association of the citizens could then take the place of the individual authority of the nobles, and the state would be protected both from tyranny and from license.

—Alexis de Tocqueville, 1835

Democratic individualism stands upon two pillars: the civil culture of rights and the political culture of the equal dignity of persons. The long-term history of the political culture of rights began with the seventeenth- and eighteenth-century revolutions against the absolutist monarchies fought in the name of, and by means of, a constitutional strategy founded upon the division of powers and the claim that electoral consent was the basis for creating legitimate governments. The descendants of Adam and Eve, wrote John Lilburne in 1646, are and forever were "by nature all equal and alike in power, dignity, authority, and majesty, none of them having by nature any authority, dominion or magisterial power one over or above another."[1] The short-term history of the political culture of equal dignity, the one that impacts most directly upon our everyday life, was largely affirmed in the aftermath of the Second World War, when constitutional democracy emerged as a model of free government in countries in which political power had been used to implement communitarian purity and exclude those who did not fit in—for reasons of race, political ideology, or sexual orientation.

In this short-term history, as in the long-term one, a reaction against absolutist and, indeed, tyrannical regimes was involved; in addition, against new forms of criminal and totalitarian despotism that were imposed through the manipulation of consent and the mobilization of the masses, not only by violence and repression. As Norberto Bobbio wrote in 1946 by way of a comment upon his inaugural lecture, delivered at the University of Padua in the aftermath of the war, "I chose the theme 'The Person and the State,' whereby democracy was presented as the form of government that is based upon respect for the human person, against every form of totalitarianism."[2]

These two histories—longer and shorter term—do not run in parallel but intersect, because they take their inspiration from the same principle, the one that has been well explained by Anna Elisabetta Galeotti: equal respect "gave value and significance to the liberal demand for *equal liberties* and to the democratic one for *equal participation* in the building of the political community."[3] They testify to the fact that the affirmation of a culture that links the power of the state to respect for the judgment of citizens (the vote) and for the moral and juridical dignity of each individual (fundamental rights) has radically altered human relationships and the mode itself of formulating moral judgments. Although never "fully realized" or even subject to a single, standard interpretation, the ideal of the dignity of the individual has become the most radical challenge to political and social institutions, which can no longer pretend to ignore it, even if they might (and in many countries do) violate it.[4] It has inaugurated a never completed or stabilized movement of demands for new rights or new inclusions, but also of contestation and resistance to the con- stituted power, irrespective of whether it is legitimized by the opinion of a majority that has been elected or imposed by the arbitrary will of a monarch. The first conclusion that we can draw from this cursory reconnaissance is that democracy is the political order which is best disposed and predisposed to treat individuals as free and equal.

This maxim could be rendered in the form of a hypo- thetical imperative: "If you wish to treat individuals as free and equal you must opt for democracy." The implications are two- fold: first of all, anyone who rejects democracy is presumably also convinced that not all persons deserve respect because, in her or his view, not all persons are equal; and second, both liberty and equality are artificial conditions, and they are not found in nature, although the religious and the philosophical arguments for human rights have done important ideological work in entrenching the idea that rights are human and even natural, and hence facilitating the transition of modern societies toward constitutional democracy.[5] This artificiality bears out the fact that both these values and democracy are acquisitions that are never guaranteed or shielded from risk. Furthermore, it sustains the conviction, shared by almost all contemporary theorists of democracy, that channeling one's behavior according to these principles (and the norms and procedures embodying them) is a permanent educational activity that serves to reinforce institutions and laws from within.

One way of distinguishing between democracy and other conceptions of free government, such as republicanism and liberalism, is to ask how such an educational activity may be attained, and who its agents might be. By contrast with republicanism, democracy does not make virtue the guiding principle of public life; as we shall see in the final chapter, educative or civic action is indirect, and is relayed through the ordinary working of political procedures and the practice of respect, which, thanks to rights, regulates interpersonal relations. Finally, by contrast with liberalism, democracy assigns a central role to the forms of political participation, both those that concern the taking of decisions regarding laws (voting for representatives or parties or in referenda), and those that are expressed through the public presence of ideas and in the formation and manifestation of political opinions. I shall enlarge upon these differences in the course of the present book.

In the Western democracies, the 1960s and 1970s (the years serving to define the short-term history under discussion here) inaugurated the age of civil rights, enabling millions of citizens to experience in their private and social life the effects of legal equality and of political rights; they assigned to civil rights the function of making democratic life a practice of recognition of individual differences, and included among the public goods to be enjoyed equitably respect and dignity. Civil and social rights thereby acquired a metajuridical significance; they have become a sign and a condition of cultural liberation, of the emancipation of everyday life from economic obstacles but also from the snares represented by authoritarian and hierarchical traditions and values. They have demonstrated their markedly individualistic implications. And it is indeed in the name of the individual and of equality of respect that they are demanded, proclaimed, and used: from the right to dissolve the marriage contract and to experience maternity by choice and responsibly, to the right to decide whom one is to live with as a couple and in marriage, or, finally, to the right to choose if and how to believe in God, if and with whom to associate in order to resolve social problems or to share cultural and religious practices.

The culture of rights is individualistic in its foundations also, when it is invoked in order to devise identitary arguments and defend identitary traditions and even when its universalism is contested on the basis of gender or cultural differences, because it is in the name of equal respect for concrete and distinct persons (women and men who express themselves through languages, life choices, or specific cultural traditions) that difference is invoked. Not only is it legitimate to demand and to defend these rights, it is likewise legitimate to resist the attempts that are periodically made to curtail them or to impose an anti-individualistic interpretation upon them, as privileges of those who already enjoy them and in the specific forms in which they enjoy them, or as rights of a cultural and political majority that happens to live on a given territory, as exclusive goods of the members of a group deliberately imagined as a *prius* with respect to the wider political society, national and international. These communitarian and identitarian twists upon democratic culture are frequent and yet aberrant, being often a sign of intolerant visions that confuse might with right, the exercise of political functions with their possession, and democratic practices and procedures with some substantive outcomes they allow a majority to achieve. They may, moreover, be signs of another distortion well worth investigation.

Particularly in countries like Italy, which do not have a religious culture readily predisposed to embrace the individualism of rights and an ethics of respect for the sovereignty of the individual over her or his moral choices, and in which church authority gives the lead regarding judgments on right and wrong in subjective morality, the affirmation of civil rights has tended to bring to light the following paradox: it has emancipated individuals from preexisting social, authoritarian, and hierarchical snares but has not consolidated new ties consistent with the culture of rights; it has not produced the sort of ethical cement capable of binding together a society of autonomous individuals. Emancipation from the strictures of an authoritarian morality has produced a practice of liberty as license and a vision of individual liberty as antisocial individualism. To revert to Tocqueville, the culture of rights, while it humanizes politics, may give rise to a society of dissociated individuals: one that on the one hand exalts the value of each person but on the other renders a person more exposed to the accidents of life because isolated and more alone in facing up to both economic and social challenges and the power of political majorities and public opinion. Mass media populism and the resurgence of communitarian identities (that is, ethnocentric regionalism in several European countries) may find fertile ground in a liberal society in which democratic politics does not rely upon and give rise to a moral culture rendering citizens capable, for example, of distinguishing between liberty and the preponderance of private interests, and of resisting the temptation to regard these latter as a passport to the acquisition of goods, such as political power, education, and health, which, unlike other marketable commodities, should not be distributed according to the criterion of profit.

How is one to dissociate an individualism of this type from democratic individualism without straying toward communitarian and organicist solutions, or without relaunching the ethical state in one guise or another? In attempting to frame an answer to this question, we would do well to recall the fact that, as Michael Walzer has written, justice in a liberal society is the art of establishing boundaries and protecting the pluralism of spheres of life.[6] But what argument should be used to stake out the boundaries between "the spheres" or, to use a less spatial analogy, the domains? Walzer relies upon democracy, an argument that hinges either upon liberty (the division of the domains of life is under the aegis of tolerance and noncoercion) or upon the equality of citizenship (the equality of citizens who share determinate social and cultural goods and who participate in the framing of the laws by means of which their *meaning* and their mode of *distribution* are discussed, contested, and established). Democracy is therefore the more effective road for practicing the art of limiting power, the art of establishing the boundaries between the domains of life, without curtailing the equal distribution of the political power to participate in the decision-making process. Within this *culture of the limit* there may be sustenance for an individualist society that is not a zero degree of sociality but rather permits its diffusion in a multiplicity of diversified forms. The loss of authoritarian or hierarchical ties that the triumph of the civil law and rights over existential identity has sanctioned is accompanied by the formation of other, new ties and other, new forms of belonging; indeed, the forms of belonging imagined as traditional and ancestral are themselves the fruit of redefinitions of sociality that stem from their being intended to be a source of meaning for the individual.[7]

In the course of the short-term history that concerns us here, of the two partners that go to make up the government of the moderns, liberalism and democracy, it is the first that has acquired greater theoretical and ideal depth. Cold War liberalism theorized the culture of individual rights as a culture capable by itself of guaranteeing the foundations of liberty, as liberty "from" politics. Democracy has thereby been restricted in its meaning to a technique and a method of selection and replacement of the political class, as Winston Churchill's well-known definition makes plain: "No one pretends that democracy is perfect. . . . Indeed, it has been said that democracy is the worst form of government except for all those other forms that have been tried from time to time."[8] This maxim has left its mark on the interpretation of democracy in the short-term history at issue here; it rests upon the combination of imperfection and utility. Democracy is thus deemed to be imperfect inasmuch as its value is not held to lie in the achievements it allows, which often leave much to be desired, but conversely is reckoned to be useful in that, thanks to a system of rights and a written constitution, the power of the majority can be limited so as to guarantee the liberty of each to make their own choices without suffering interference on the part of the state for reasons that go beyond the primary concern to ensure the security that is common to all. This has been the main tenet of liberal democracy in the decades of the Cold War. It was concerned essentially with the rules of the game and the neutral functioning of the administration of the state. Fundamentally important though this maxim may be, it nonetheless does not say that democracy is also the only imperfect form of government which allows citizens to recognize and denounce, openly and publicly, its imperfection; which, in other words, lives off political participation, direct and indirect, by means of the vote and public judgment. It would be wholly fitting to supplement Churchill's maxim with that of Niccolò Machiavelli: "This sentiment against the people arises because everyone speaks badly about the people without fear and in complete freedom even while the people rule."[9] Criticizing the holders of power without fear and openly is the disposition that best describes the democratic individual (the Athenians considered *parrhēsia*—speaking out freely and bluntly—a virtue); it is, as we shall see in the conclusion to the present book, the characteristic that is expressed in dissent, the virtue of the moderns.

Democracy is good not by dint of the outcomes that it enables one to obtain (majority decisions are not always or necessarily the best or the wisest) but because its procedures, rules, and institutions are conceived in such a fashion as to render all laws open to criticism and revision on the part of those who must obey them. One could say that it is a process of permanent change, because it presumes that imperfection pertains to all human beings without exception; for this reason democracy denotes an earthly temporality, and is itself a site of mutability. Which is why freedom of speech and the unfettered expression of dissent, taking part in the process of deliberation in an indirect or a direct form, are essential to democracy, while they are also an explicit acknowledgment of their pragmatic functionality, inasmuch as they ensure that any failings that we may individually have can be remedied by means of cooperation. "Ordinarily understood as an invitation to forbearance for an occasional mistake," the saying *errare humanum est* "can be totally reinterpreted to mean that mistake-making is an exclusive *faculty* of humans. In other words, the meaning of the saying is not 'to err is only human' but 'only humans err.' "[10] The capacity "to make mistakes" is the hallmark of the freedom to choose and of our consequent responsibilities. By the same token it is the condition that renders democratic government human and "rational," since it entails, as we have already noted, the possibility of combining different competences on an equal and cooperative footing in order to decide upon questions that concern a collectivity of individuals. Democracy does not therefore ask to be considered the best of all possible regimes. Rather, it requires citizens to recognize their own permanent work of changeability, a recognition that is at one and the same time the logical premise and the practical outcome of the acceptance of the rule of the majority. From which there derives the "need" to be free to associate in order to seek solutions to the problems that they themselves raise. From which there also derives the fact that, despite repeated attempts to interpret political deliberation syllogistically, it always involves probability and a method that proceeds by trial and error. Its logic may be illustrated by the strategy used by the Plataeans and Athenians, when besieged by the Peloponnesians and the Boeotians, in order to realize mass flight. Thucydides tells of how, having decided to make ladders that would enable them to scale the enemy walls, and needing to know the exact height of the walls, they placed their trust in the principle of number and of the majority (better the cooperation of so many than the eyes of one): "A great many counted at once, and although some might make mistakes, the calculation would be oftener right than wrong; for they repeated the process again and again, and, the distance not being great, they could see the wall distinctly enough for their purpose. In this manner they ascertained the proper length of the ladders, taking as a measure the thickness of the bricks."[11] Individual responsibility, knowledge, transparency, cooperation for a common enterprise, dissent, and the possibility of ratifying decisions taken are the essential components of the democratic method of making decisions, a method that expresses two "natural" ideas for the individual, which are interlinked: that of being free to act "on his own" and that of "combining his efforts with those of his fellows and acting together."[12]

As we shall see in chapter 9, this perspective is founded upon the idea of voluntary engagement. For this reason democracy has been equated with a "voluntary scheme of cooperation,"[13] a definition that captures very effectively the characteristic of democratic autonomy as a peculiarity of a political order that has no elsewhere. If democracy does not have an elsewhere, this is not in a theological sense but for intrinsic reasons touching upon its very nature; reasons that may be summed up under three headings, all pertaining to the category of political autonomy.[14] First of all, because it is not possible (or until now has not been) to posit and create a form of government that is better than democracy, given the same conditions, or one that succeeds with a different distribution of power and different decision-making procedures in respecting individual liberty and in guaranteeing the moral, legal, and political equality, and the equality of opportunity, of all its citizens. Isaiah Berlin had argued that individual liberty (the state of not being subjected to interference from others or from the law) can be respected or violated as readily in an autocracy as in a democracy. However, Berlin never argued that one could say as much if one took as one's guiding value not simply negative liberty but an equal liberty to not be subjected to arbitrary interference. In essence, if we keep faith with the principle of liberty we cannot help but combine it with equality, yet at this point we cannot sustain the conclusion that, where liberty is concerned, an autocracy and a democracy do not entail radical differences. The second point shedding light upon the notion that democracy has no elsewhere pertains to the nature of its legitimacy, in other words, to the fact that its foundations are not outside or above it but within its actual processuality. This radical immanence, which makes of democracy the only system that can lay claim to political autonomy where citizens are concerned, has had important modern theorists, such as John Dewey and Jürgen Habermas, who have convincingly shown that democracy has no need to presuppose the existence of a prepolitical nature, the seat of inalienable human rights, in order to justify and respect those rights. On the contrary, democracy manifests itself (its history begins) precisely when a community creates the instrument of right with which to resolve its internal conflicts and to regulate its public relationships. There is no democracy existing independently of individual liberty and of those rights that we call fundamental—the one implies the other, and vice versa, if it is true that in democracy politics is forged from the open, plural, and public expression of opinions, a dialectical forum in which only consent can emerge (or change) and in which dissent has full entitlement. Finally, and as a third point correlated with the first two, in no political system is it so crucial that means and ends are not at odds: policies and governments cannot be changed through the agency of the vote and of an election without civil liberties at the same time being respected and without there being a foundation of equality (that this latter is more or less complete in its realization is a historical and empirical fact that does not alter the egalitarian foundation of legitimacy through express and free consent upon which this government is founded). Democracy is means and end; and if it does not allow loopholes or shortcuts it is because it is not simply a functional method for attaining a goal determined externally to its own process. Of the two partners, liberalism and democracy, it is therefore fitting that we turn our attention to the second, the more political of the two, though with the proviso that the minimalist conception of democracy needs to be revised in order to be better defended. This conception arose through liberals' justified mistrust of the militant demagoguery characterizing the totalitarianisms of the twentieth century. But in our posttotalitarian democracies—participants in a global order that renders normative, economic, and cultural borders ever more labile and hard to discern or patrol—this minimalist vision, apart from being insufficient, may become an obstacle to the diagnosis of the problem.

Indeed, it is not so much democratic procedures that are at issue in this historical phase of the mature democracies. The theme under dispute is rather the definition of the identity of "who" is or should be part of the body politic, of who is admitted to use those procedures. As in the eighteenth-century phase of democratization, the definition of the sovereign body is today the most pressing problem, albeit for a new reason, and, if one may put it like this, the fruit of the social progress also set in motion by democracy in the course of the past two centuries. It is not monarchical tyranny or caste inequalities that are in question but rather the national belonging on the basis of which the democratic sovereign has defined its own constitutive identity and which has been sorely tried by factors of a transnational kind, such as migrations and economic and financial interdependence. The problem that modern democracy faces (in Europe itself, moreover) is in essence cultural and ethical rather than procedural. The posttotalitarian democracies therefore need to recover the ethical force of the dignity of the person and of reasoned participation in political life in order to shield themselves from the temptations of an intolerant communitarianism, but also to redeem the public sphere from the quasi-tyrannical sway of a possessive and politically apathetic individualism. Only thus can such polities hope to reassert and defend two of the founding values of democracy, namely, citizenship and equality.

If the posttotalitarian democracies need to recover the value of citizenship, it is for reasons of prudence and following a logic that is above all consequentialist: because the erosion of transparency in institutional action and the decline in the monitoring and surveillance of participation tend to aggravate the inequality of political power, so that those with the most economic resources can have a louder voice and a more prominent political profile, and furnish themselves with more instruments serving to mold and win consent. The same is true of the reasons justifying the reassertion of the value of equality: because the decline in policies of redistribution and social justice exacerbate the decline in equal respect, and foster a sense that participation is irrelevant. Policies of redistribution and policies of recognition are intertwined because the penalization that derives from unequal access to resources is not only material in nature but also moral and psychological.[15] Perhaps the most macroscopic example of the lengths to which a democratic government can go in reducing citizenship and equality to a minimum is supplied by the antialtruistic inflexion to which federalism has been subjected in Italy, where in recent years it has been construed as a policy of economic and cultural secession on the part of the richest regions and an abrogation of their responsibilities toward the general public or the nation.

The difference between Italians from the North and Italians from the South is not exhaustively defined by the issue of unequal material wealth or income but touches upon the distribution of an immaterial good of crucial importance for persons and for a democratic society, in short, dignity, the possibility of enjoying an equal recognition for what one is. Moral equality and existential equality converge, George Kateb writes, "on the fundamental conviction that the rights of every person are absolute, or have the presumption of absoluteness, because every person is of an absolute value."[16] This is the good under attack with a communitarian reappropriation of democracy, in the guise of a government that seeks to use majority rule to further one specific majority in particular, be it regional, religious, or purportedly ethnic.

Democracy is not only a form of government; it is also, and above all, a rich culture of individuality. The democratic individual is similar, but not identical, to the liberal and economic individual, because she is not thought of as a purely rational being who chooses between different options in a hypothetical condition of perfect information and liberty, nor even as a neutral individual, devoid of cultural, economic, or gender specificities. Rather, she is a person who has a moral sense of her own autonomy and dignity, and who in acting is swayed by passions and emotions as powerful as reasons and interests are; who is not only focused on her own endeavors but is also emotionally attuned to others for the most diverse reasons, such as empathy, curiosity, the will to imitate, the pleasure of experimenting.

These conflicting qualities have the capacity to generate unpleasant phenomena, such as an uncritical adherence to the most widely shared tastes or the burying of individual judgment in the opinion of the majority, or the imitative adherence to intolerant and discriminatory models of behavior. Nonetheless they have a positive side, one that deserves to be emphasised and even celebrated: they render the individual naturally prone to respond to others, capable of associating, of feeling a sympathetic proximity with someone different, of identifying with someone in need, of cooperating out of a calculation of utility but also for the sheer pleasure of it; finally, of feeling an imaginative proximity, as Immanuel Kant would have put it, with all human beings, even those who are distant and far removed from our own history, with predictable universalistic implications. We are concerned here with *transcendental* qualities that give meaning and value to equality and enable us to distinguish democratic individualism from other forms of individualistic affirmation; and, above all, with qualities, first and foremost that of cooperation, whose existence was not dreamed up by the idealists of democracy but has in fact been borne out by experimental evidence. Political action and ideologies can propel democracy in one direction or the other. The populist and the communitarian right have proved capable of turning the characteristics of individualism to their own advantage, bringing to light its more vulgar, mass, and apathetic aspect. In this book I have set out to show how this interpretation is skewed and contradicts the very foundations of democracy.

II

Private Happiness

Citizenship, in free countries, is partly a school of society in equality; but citizenship fills only a small place in modern life, and does not come near the daily habits or inmost sentiments.

—*John Stuart Mill, 1869*

A s a political category, "individualism" is polemical in its character and meaning. As I shall explain in the next chapter, this category was originally employed to express a negative state of society and, consequently, of the individual: a condition of tyrannical egoism, atomism, anarchy, and social disintegration. In this guise the term made its appearance in post-Napoleonic Europe among conservatives, republicans, and even liberals, subsequently becoming from the end of the nineteenth century onward perhaps the object most studied by sociologists, who sought to understand how it was possible for a society of individuals to cohere, and how it was that from individualism solidarity might issue—to paraphrase Émile Durkheim, who, much like Tocqueville, thought that in reality "not only is individualism distinct from anarchy; but it is henceforth the only system of beliefs which can ensure the moral unity of the country."[1]

Yet the most important aspect of the success of the individualistic ethos is represented by its direct relation to the expansion of the private dimension of human existence, not simply inasmuch as it is distinct from the political dimension, but also inasmuch as it is to the detriment of, and opposed to, it. The first theorist to elucidate this point, and in impeccable style, was Benjamin Constant, in his famous discourse on the liberty of the moderns compared with that of the ancients, delivered at the Athénée royal in 1819.[2] Constant's account of the difference between ancients and moderns hinged precisely upon the individual dimension of existence. The former, he said, knew and pursued public happiness, whereas the latter were almost exclusively concerned with private happiness ("la jouissance de notre indépendance privée"). The ancients esteemed a type of pleasure to which the moderns were seemingly impervious: the sort that derived from participating actively and directly in the life of the city, discussing and approving laws, judging those who were in breach of them, exposing themselves in speech to the judgment of others, and, finally, being ready to fight and to sacrifice their own lives if the city demanded it. Moreover, the interests of the city were identical with their interests, since the citizens of the ancient republics were the owners of the land that they ruled: fighting against external enemies or conquering new territory in order to defend their own was an integral part of their political liberty because a reason for their survival (and a circumstance that led Constant to mistrust the myth of the ancients). Be that as it may, living in public rather than simply for the public was a condition scholars from Constant to Hannah Arendt had associated with the classical world.

The moderns, according to this dyadic interpretation, which has proved so extraordinarily influential as much in the political sciences as in sociology, were attracted by a different kind of pleasure: the sort that stems from independence, from the quiet life lived in the midst of family and friends, from the satisfaction of enriching oneself, and finally from the solitary life itself; from everything that is distant not only from the din of the public square but above all from the active exercise of politics. Not that the ancients were unacquainted with the world of individuality—Cicero has left us eminently modern pages on the many pleasures that he derived from private and domestic life, on the sweetness of friendship, on the unquenchable desire to flee the Forum and to immerse himself instead in reading simply for its own sake. The fact is that for the ancients the private dimension, although cherished and even yearned after, did not represent an ideal of life; if it possessed value, it was because the city had a healthy and vibrant political life; because civil and political liberty were not at risk and citizens were active in promoting it and in protecting it from external enemies and from internal ones too, first and foremost, corruption. Finally, the recognition of one's peers and a sense of self-esteem derived from the practice of public business and direct involvement in politics through eloquence or war: such, for the ancients, was the richest source of personal happiness.

In a series of memorable pages Hannah Arendt has reminded us that from the moment that, with the advent of Christianity, the quest for salvation and for the immortality of the soul had become the goal of the person, life on this earth and in the city began to be lived as an obstacle or at most as a brute necessity, at any event, a condition not of happiness but of sacrifice and of need and in this sense a sign of veritable imperfection. With the advent of this conception of liberty as liberty from politics, the human world changed radically, and not only the private but also the public world, because it led individuals to identify politics with the means to obtain personal security and the security of possessions, with the machinery of institutions. From being an art of public discourse and an activity pursued for public ends, politics has become a science of the preservation of the state as an order, a question of technical certainties and truths, increasingly the preserve of experts and far removed therefore from the discourse of the ordinary citizens, who are never deemed sufficiently competent. The dichotomy between city (it would be better to say "state") and politics has been the most conspicuous consequence of the demise of the classical world, and with it the recasting of the public dimension as a site of individual fulfillment.[3]

In this interpretation, modernity begins with Christianity, and above all with humanism. The quest for the solitary life that inspired Francesco Petrarch and the Italian humanists was as modern a thing as could be imagined in an age in which the values of civil life were so far from being spontaneous that they had to be instilled in the hearts of men from childhood through the reading of history books and of tales of the exemplary lives of the ancients; noteworthy attempts at education that revealed the artificiality of these ideals, fragile in the face of the rivalry of the more spontaneous economic interests or of the pleasures associated with private life.[4] The free Italian cities in the period of humanism had taken the names for the institutions and the republican offices from the classical world, imitated ancient models of eloquence, embraced the rhetoric of virtue and glory; but their citizens were often inept military men, displaying little bravery as soldiers, and were instead active entrepreneurs, men of business who produced goods to trade, sought markets outside the walls, opened banking branches in distant foreign cities, owned properties wherever it was convenient, and preferred to delegate through election the "affairs" of government so as to be more able to devote themselves to their own.[5]

Jacob Burckhardt spoke of the Italians of the trecento and the quattrocento as being to all intents and purposes moderns ("the Italian ... was the firstborn among the sons of modern Europe") not only because they were reluctant to sacrifice themselves to active politics or to go to war but also because in their world of values everything involving the private individual took precedence over whatever concerned the citizen.[6] Their republics were short-lived and turbulent, and tyranny prevailed more or less everywhere, as if to show how hard it was for the union between "public happiness" and "private happiness" to endure. Even when their republics achieved greatness and were admired as such, the pursuit and exercise of power were cultivated for personal gratification or, as Constant put it, in order to satisfy a wholly private desire, that is, to win, to be admired, to accumulate more power, to dominate others.

For Montesquieu, by whom Constant had been inspired when formulating his own distinction between ancients and moderns, the Italian republics of the quattrocento were therefore not good republics and in reality were nearer to being despotic governments, because simply in order to endure they had to induce their own citizens to do what for them was an increasingly less spontaneous thing to do: to participate in the public life of the city for the good of the city and not directly for their own. The author of *The Spirit of the Laws* had on the one hand endorsed the intuition once articulated by Machiavelli, to the effect that republican virtues clash with Christian ones, and on the other hand he had maintained, unlike Machiavelli, that the virtues of the ancients were lost once and for all; the moderns had heard tell of them, but they had never experienced them. They were literary virtues, not ones that were enacted. Whereas Machiavelli had believed that knowledge of the classics could bring virtue and heroism back to life through emulation and imitation, Montesquieu seemed to be telling his readers that the more they studied the classics, the more they would come to realize how impossible (and undesirable) it was to emulate them. Civic virtue had succeeded in sustaining liberty for so long as individualism was not sufficiently robust. But in the Italian cities of the Renaissance civic virtue would inevitably topple over into tyranny because, since society did not produce such a virtue naturally, politics had necessarily to impose it with the instruments of coercion and force, or the intellectuals had to propagandize for it with the weapons of literature and eloquence. So far as Montesquieu was concerned, those republics were proof of the anachronistic nature of the classical political model transplanted into a society that, like the modern, was dependent upon trade and exchange rather than upon military conquest: if they were easy prey to unscrupulous *signori* this was because these modern tyrants expressed the values and way of life of the society of their own time far better than the austere republican institutions of antiquity did.[7] They were a representation, albeit an exaggerated one, of the moral culture of their fellow citizens: like them they practiced the arts and trade, loved wealth and luxury, family and literary life, and were loath to commit themselves to public service, so much so that they turned it into a private affair.

One reason for the difference between the ancients and moderns in their manner of evaluating private life, Constant and Arendt reckoned, was the fact that for the ancients life in

the family and in the economy was directly associated with
slavery and a despotic dependence upon need and labor, and
not with a free relationship with and between equals. What sort
of happiness could stem from the *oikos*? That is not how it was
with the moderns. Although women were, and would continue
to be for several centuries to come, not political companions
but the devoted servants of men, nonetheless in the economic
world slavery had been abolished in the Italian cities of the
humanist period, where labor began to be associated with
money and with paid service, subject like other goods to the
market, and no longer the preserve of slaves. Subsequently,
labor gradually became a means to prosperity but also a condition of liberty and personal fulfillment, and no longer a mark
of dependence opposed to *otium*; this did much to emancipate
society and individuals from despotic relationships and to
nurture the idea of equality of conditions, which was followed
by that of conceiving of politics as a means to acquire social
security and rights.

    "In the other countries of Europe, the different classes of
society lived apart, each with its own medieval caste sense of
honour. . . . But in Italy social equality had appeared before the
time of the tyrannies or the democracies. We there find early
traces of a general society."[8] Burckhardt's words bear a marked
similarity to those used by Tocqueville to describe nineteenth-
century America. In the Italian cities of the humanist period,
as in the townships of New England Tocqueville visited and
admired, two forces were in play: equality of conditions and
the market economy, both held together by Christianity, an
ethics of salvation, indeed, but also an ethics of labor serving
to express God-given talents, the nurturing of the self and of
the family. In both cases, the private and individual dimension
was a cardinal value, being accorded precedence hierarchically

over the public dimension, although its flourishing might nonetheless depend upon this latter, or, in other words, upon good laws and sound institutional *ordini*.

One should therefore say that private and public were not so much opposed as in a state of fruitful tension. At any rate such was the interpretation Arendt sought to give of the difference between ancients and moderns. Arendt maintained that the appearance with Christianity of the priority of the inner life over the outer, of the eternal over the earthly, served as a sort of premonition of highly distinctive risks, those that might potentially arise with the transformation of politics into a means allowing men to pursue a goal superior to, or transcending, politics. From this overturning of politics, whereby it became a means to acquire private happiness, was born the idea of politics as a technique of power, the handmaiden of instrumentalist and utilitarian reason, conforming to a model of the individual that reflected the paradigm of *homo oeconomicus*, an agent selecting from preferences assumed as given. Once it had been transformed into a question of functional rationality, identified with necessity but not with a value, a site of obedience rather than of free public activity, modern politics was destined to engender the following contradiction: though it first arose in order to shield the private dimension of interests and affects, its technicist and instrumental configuration, and the devaluation it has suffered, have led to its endangering the very thing it was supposed to protect.

The advent of modern democracy, from the eighteenth century onward, has thus been framed by a dichotomy between modernity construed as a culture of individuality (and therefore of rights) and modernity cast as individualism and as the technique of power (that of the economy or that of the state). Individualism is therefore a polemical category, and not only because, as we shall see in the next chapter, it was coined historically with this purpose in mind but also because of its intrinsic nature. The opposite of individualism is not simply a communitarian and inegalitarian society, nor is it merely the ancien régime or antimodernity, although this had been the view of its first radical critics. An alternative to the ideology of individualism might also be a moral and political culture of respect for the individual, for his rights and for his fundamental equality. Individualism is therefore a complex term that designates a way of conceiving the public world and its relationship with the private one; and it can be subversive not only of a world structured through hierarchies but also of a way of conceiving modern society that regards the public sphere as a domain in which rules and institutions are created and choices evaluated which predispose citizens to share goods (respect and rights), to respect each other even when interests and ideas are at odds, to seek neither a flight from politics nor indeed the abuse of politics for their own ends, be they a matter of personal power or of private interest. The fact that politics helps to create a world in which the individual pursues private happiness does not necessarily constitute an invitation to its instrumentalization. The theme of individualism is therefore complex, and not reducible to a struggle for and against the centrality of the individual, for and against modern society, for and against communitarian values. I propose here to consider individualism as the other face of the political order rather than its opposite, in the sense that the perspective from which one evaluates and practices politics is a reflected image of the mode of thinking and being of individualism. It is fitting therefore at this point to proceed to differentiate between the various forms of individualism, and above all to analyze and understand the crisis of public ethics in contemporary democracy.

III

An "Ism" to Be Used
with Caution

Once the concrete individual has been removed from his individual
"history" there is a risk of him dwindling to a mere metaphysical
possibility.

—*Giulio Preti, 1957*

I ndividualism is an "ism," and for this reason all too prone
to simplifications that tend to mask the different ideological elements of which it is composed or to exalt some
of them above others. A great historian of ideas, Arthur
Lovejoy, has suggested that we handle "isms" with caution, and
think of them as chemical compounds or *unit-ideas* that
combine under a single term a number of distinct doctrines
which, if considered separately, are often in conflict.[1] If we

apply Lovejoy's suggestion to the analysis of individualism, we find that it contains at least four distinct families of doctrines, religious, political, philosophical, and economic. As religious individualism, individualism may be equated with the principle of "free examination" asserted by Martin Luther against and in reaction to the ecclesiastical hierarchy. His famous maxim "sola fide, sola gratia, sola scriptura" renders individual conscience (though certainly illuminated by faith) sovereign in the world because in a direct relationship with God. The divinity of man, which is manifested in his spiritual liberty (unlimited and pure) from worldliness, and his ineluctable needs (nature but also the sphere of the emotions) are what define individuality as a supreme value, or what confer upon the person the responsibility to testify through his own life to the divinity that is in him. This religion is at one and the same time individualist and rooted in the community, because the Christian obligation that every believer has to honor his God-given talents, by putting them into practice, presupposes a community of reference that is able to recognize, respect, put to the best possible uses, and reward these same talents. Without a society with which there is a sympathetic correspondence of values there is no wholly fulfilled individual life. It is no accident that among the first revolutionary innovations of the Reformation was the abolition of celibacy, a state of inegalitarian separation within the community between the class of ministers and their congregations; from this there followed the sanctification of earthly life and labor as signs of the manifestation of the divine.[2] The description proposed by Kant of the human condition as one of "unsociable sociability"[3] stems from this same religious individualism, which historically has become the ethical and moral foundation of the liberty of the moderns or, as Montesquieu has suggested, of the liberty born in Northern Europe.

Inasmuch as it implies the egalitarian theory of human rights, individualism has, moreover, been recognized to be a central element in political liberalism. John Dewey wrote that "accidental inequalities of birth, wealth and learning are always tending to restrict the opportunities of some as compared with those of others" and maintained that a just society is one that works to remove the obstacles represented by time and by chance: by history (social capital and economic inequality) and by nature (physical handicap or age).[4] The justification for this action of politics to correct history and nature lies in the recognition of the equal value of individuals. The same idea informs the liberalism of John Rawls, who, when in *A Theory of Justice* he settles upon the principles and procedures of justice that are designed to correct the "unequal inheritance of wealth" and strip "circumstances, institutions and historical traditions" of their power, revives the theme of the struggle of law against the sedimentations of society and the vicissitudes of nature in the name of the value upon which liberalism and the idea of the just society rests, namely, "reasonable human autonomy."[5]

This is why the culture of rights does not necessarily translate as a containment of politics, for whereas this culture does indeed have a negative conception of individual liberty as freedom from interference, it is at the same time also concerned with the opportunities that liberty has to develop. By contrast with Rawls, a more explicit acknowledgment of the social and reformist implications of the liberty of the moderns is evident in Amartya Sen, who proposes a revision in an Aristotelian sense of individualist culture, since on the one hand he insists upon individual choice as the yardstick of liberty and on the other brings into play the idea of happiness as a flourishing of the person, with respect to which free choice has a decisive function. Justice is therefore evaluated not only from the point of view of the treatment accorded by institutions or by political power (rules of justice) but also from the point of view of the ethical and cultural ties which bind the individual to society and which create what has been termed an "atmosphere" of liberty, the wider context in which individual choices take on meaning. The development of the individual capacities here replaces opportunities in the evaluation of justice.[6]

Liberalism, according to Sen, should not simply provide for the identification of the rules and procedures that allow institutions to treat individuals fairly but ought also to pay attention to the concrete social and cultural conditions in which individual choice occurs, conditions which may weaken or enrich capacities, which may render personal efforts to pursue individual projects fruitless or rather effective and gratifying. Sen shifts the focus from external conditions (institutions, norms, procedures) to the development of the capacities that in a specific society enable the individual to operate in a fashion furthering his own expectations, with the result that he is happy or aware of his own well-being or, conversely, conscious of his own malaise and of what is necessary to overcome it.[7]

Setting aside the simple abstract or normative concept of the individual, Sen proposes to seek out the qualitative parameters by which to measure the degree of liberty as capacity, parameters operating with variables capable of interpreting social specificity; which could, for example, interpret poverty not simply on the basis of income but in terms of the effective resources, material and human, that a person needs in his society for his action to be an effective cause of well-being. Being illiterate in a rich and advanced society is different from being such in a developing society, not only because, in order to function effectively, a person must, in the former case, bring into play many more knowledges and capacities but also because in advanced societies deprivation is invariably accompanied by negative sentiments (it is a stigma) that aggravate the plight of the indigent person and render her less able psychologically and morally to make the best possible use of her own energies or will, in short, less free.[8] Nonetheless, both the liberalism that hinges upon the institutions and procedures that regulate social relations with a view to rendering them fair and just (Rawls) and the kind that turns upon individual liberty as a functional capacity for action (Sen) are philosophical and political expressions of a liberal perspective that is individualist and egalitarian.

In the case of the third family of doctrines, the philosophical, individualism may be identified with romantic individualism. For romantic individualism, the differences between individuals are perhaps more important than equality, whether points of departure (spiritual potentialities) are involved or ultimate goals. Here individuality fosters uniqueness, but also inequality. Jean-Jacques Rousseau, the inspiration behind this form of individualism, thought that all human beings were naturally different and that precisely in order to ensure that this diversity remained a natural difference and did not become a reason for an inequality in esteem and power it was necessary to construct a government of society based upon law deriving from and applying to all equally. In order for individuals who were different and often unequal in their physical qualities to live together as equals they were therefore supposed not to nullify their concrete differences (and certainly not their personal ones) but to render them inoperative when it was a matter of making and obeying civil laws. From this important correlation between difference and equality nineteenth-century liberalism took shape, or at any rate that of Wilhelm von Humboldt and John Stuart Mill, for whom the culture of individuality—that of the "sovereignty of the individual"—springs naturally from the freedom of action and the greater intrinsic diversity of individuals.[9] Liberty, individuality, and pluralism are here inseparable.

Nonetheless, the rift between nature and artifice has also inspired a romanticism that is not egalitarian. Its classical inspiration has been found in the disjuncture between laws of nature and laws of society discussed by, for example, Plato in a dialogue which has loomed large in the history of Western thought and in which Callicles was the protagonist. In the *Gorgias*, in an exchange with Socrates, Callicles issued a message that would have gladdened the hearts of the liberal individualists of the nineteenth century: being sincere with oneself cannot help but enter into conflict with the opinion of others; when this occurs, the value of the individual and of his ideas takes precedence: "Yet, I think, my good sir, that it would be better for me to have a musical instrument or a chorus which I was directing in discord and out of tune, better that the mass of mankind should disagree with me and contradict me than that I, a single individual, should be out of harmony with myself and contradict myself."[10] Ralph Waldo Emerson, Henry Thoreau, Wilhelm von Humboldt, and John Stuart Mill have recast this maxim very effectively in their own writings. The dualism between individual liberty in ideas and in lifestyles and the tyranny of public opinion was one of their constant preoccupations. They would demonstrate how, on this theme, liberalism and romantic philosophy converged. However, as regards the message of the second exchange between Callicles and Socrates, these liberal authors were very far from being in agreement.

Plato here has Callicles say that equality is the revenge of the law against nature. "In the natural sense anything that is a greater evil is also baser—in this case suffering wrong; but conventionally doing wrong is the baser of the two." The law of men overturns that of nature and alters the notion of good and evil because it decrees that refraining from doing harm to others and the self-repression of the passions that impel us to assert ourselves even against others should occupy the highest place in the hierarchy of values. The social law ordains that we not destroy the other, and punishes not the one who is destroyed, as nature does, but the one who prevails.[11]

Equality, Callicles suggests, supplying Friedrich Nietzsche with a formidable argument against democracy, is a social or artificial value, systematically instilled in every individual from birth so that he may become habituated in his life to despising the stronger characters and to suppressing his own genuine uniqueness. The success of democracy depends upon the success of this socialization into equality. Nietzsche in essence, and quite rightly, says that without an educative action upon the feelings (without, in other words, a molding of nature), equality tends to subside and even to disappear from the list of values, because it is the creation of society and an artificial fact that, if not cultivated, is destined to yield ground to the rule of nature, which rewards the strong and the brave and feels no compassion for those who fall by the wayside.[12] Nietzsche himself never applied this doctrine to the economic competition of capitalist and commercial society, but the free-trade theoreticians of social Darwinism and the doctrinaire advocates of a struggle between the races, on account of what they construed as the natural superiority of some of them, drew highly explicit consequences from the idea of radical inequality contained in this classical heritage that had become a component of romantic individualism.

Plainly romanticism advanced two different visions of the sovereignty of the individual, one of which found expression in the theory of democratic equality, the other in its contrary. In both cases, however, the view very clearly emerges that, to revert once again to Rousseau, the equality of the law is a creation of society and of education; being an artificial fact that has endlessly to be reproduced it may, if society fails to nurture it, cease to exist or else decline. Equality is a conquest by civilization and can fade from the hearts and minds of individuals. This is why democratic society is an educational project (although its educational effect is unpremeditated) and not merely a form of government. "The law, they say, is liberty. We acknowledge this to be true in an absolute sense . . . liberty really is in custom, in the habits of everyday life. . . . But what happens is this: the law becomes scripture, it travels, it is propagated and in being propagated it also falls into the desert. The desert is those countries in which custom is in so degraded a state that written law has no guarantee in practice. . . . A law is a living thing only insofar as it is based upon a solid custom, which guarantees it, without the need for too many bureaucratic checks."[13]

Insofar as it is the equivalent of an antistatist theory, individualism is, when all is said and done, the central nucleus of the doctrine of *economic liberalism*. Now, whereas in the case of religious individualism and in that of the kind contained within political liberalism, individualism is in a direct relationship with equality, in the case of romantic individualism, as in that of economic individualism, the relationship is oblique and can become problematic: this is the cause of the complex relationships between economic individualism and democratic individualism. Where economic individualism is concerned, indeed, equality is written into the rules of competition and into the opportunities offered by the market to receive a reward for enterprise and for personal sacrifices, according to the maxim that each is not only master of his physical and mental energies, as he is of the things that he owns and exchanges, but also the best judge of what it is good for him to do or to refrain from doing. Except for the fact that, while human faculties are potentially the same in all individuals, their degree of perfection, their specialization and their development are instead the out-come of the varying commitment of each, and likewise also of the choices and accomplishment of previous generations, so that it is difficult to find a moment of entirely equal circum-stances in which all individuals begin the competition of life on a footing of parity. But the normative nucleus of economic individualism—above all the kind consolidated from the second half of the nineteenth century onward, in conjunction with and in reaction to the growth of the social functions of the state—is that if competition is left unfettered and there is a situation of optimal information, even if the outcomes at which the in-dividuals arrive tend to be unequal one to the other, this fact will not compromise the possibility of there being a harmoni-ous and just society, because the individuals know in advance that the distribution of costs and benefits will occur on account of proven merits and through the market, and not be settled at the discretion of governments cleaving to consensus rather than to merit (a utopian vision that has inspired anarchists and libertarian socialists).[14]

The restriction upon politics, its withdrawal from the economic sphere, is here a condition of social peace and the foundation of the sentiment of justice, because, it is argued, the market distributes according to impersonal and unpolitical criteria. Hence the idea of a liberal justice which is noninter-ventionist, and which, Robert Nozick maintained, operates according to the maxim "From each as they choose, to each as they are chosen."[15]

What relationship is there between these four doctrines of individualism, and what bearing do they have upon democratic individualism? There is no doubting the fact that from the encounter between romanticism and liberalism there arose the idea that the culture of rights not only does not engender anarchy but can indeed produce a stable and united society. The primacy of "individual sovereignty" can serve to constitute the social order on more solid foundations. Here the philosophy of the individual is proposed "not in order to bring about the crisis of a universality and a community but, on the contrary, precisely to respond to such a crisis."[16] We are concerned here with a philosophy that is without a doubt related to Christian religious individualism, which advocates equality as the actual condition of the supreme value assigned to the individual by the Creator. From these premises it follows that society and its political institutions should be so directed that they promote individual dispositions, the value of which transcends the actual social and cultural conventions and is measured by the common perspective of limitation and of belonging to humanity. The individual is a unique and irreplaceable infinity, and this applies to all human beings. Though referred to Christian belonging in a general sense, this idea of universality is to be found for instance in Saint Paul's epistle to the Colossians, where we read that there are neither Greeks nor Jews nor barbarians, and that compliance with written and customary law is beside the point, because "Christ is all, and in all."

The relationship between democratic individualism and economic liberalism, crucial though it may be, is nonetheless contested. Both of these forms of individualism assign centrality to liberty and to personal responsibility, but the former is far readier than the latter to embrace the idea that government and civil society as a whole should encourage the culture of individuality through policies which do not limit themselves to not interfering with individual choices but which, by means of indirect incentives or direct interventions, also propose to correct the inevitable causes of material and social inequality that a market economy produces. So far as democratic individualism is concerned, it is not the liberty of the market that is the fundamental value but rather the actual capacity of concrete individuals to operate with autonomous responsibility in the society in which they live, a premise that may require political interventions in the economic sphere designed to promote redistribution and in the financial sphere to enhance checks and transparency.

In order to maintain a "distributional patterned principle of justice" over time—Nozick wrote—"one must either interfere continually to stop people from transferring resources as they wish to, or continually (or periodically) interfere to take from some persons resources that others for some reason choose to transfer to them." In conclusion, "no distributional patterned principle of justice can be continuously realized without continuous interference with people's life."[17] Nozick was right. The question, however, arises that if at the center there is not a simple paradigm but the concrete circumstance of men and women, the problem will then probably concern the forms of interference rather than the choice between interference and noninterference. Political interventions, as Martha Nussbaum and Amartya Sen have argued, may be multiple, assuming the form both of universalistic redistributive policies and of actions that are indirect, are in the guise of incentives and are framed in response to needs. The difference between the former and the latter stems from the attention paid by politics and economics to the concrete situation in which citizens happen to live, the prejudices and values within which is encapsulated their

freedom of choice, and the social and cultural difficulties that
are interposed between the equality of principle of which they
are the titulars (fundamental rights), or the potentiality to make
meaningful choices, and the effects these choices have upon
their personal life and relationships.[18] The "warning" issued by
Sen to the economy was that it not transform itself from a
"social science" into a "science of nature," and that it regard the
pursuit of well-being as a commitment to attaining a condition
of life that is dignified.[19]

The judgment on the forms of intervention is therefore a
judgment on means and their greater or lesser efficacy relative
to the circumstances and conditions prevailing in a given society. The goal is to consider the individual as a social actor and
a person worthy of equal respect. "Furthermore, we have to go
beyond economic growth to understand the fuller demands of
development and of the pursuit of social welfare. Attention
must be paid to the extensive evidence that democracy and
political and civil rights tend to enhance freedoms of other
kinds (such as human security) through giving a voice, at least
in many circumstances, to the deprived and the vulnerable."[20]
Economic independence, Mill maintained, is a corollary of
liberty and, as such, justifies the interference of the state and a
transformation of the legislation that regulates the social relations of property in order to "rectify" every thing that "conflicts"
with "the ends which render private property" compatible with
its own principle, which is that of "[guaranteeing] to individuals the fruits of their own labour and abstinence."[21]

IV

A Brief History of Individualism

The progress of individualism, the erosion of democratic vitality, the decline of civic sense: the same pessimistic and nostalgic diagnosis has reappeared everywhere.

—*Pierre Rosanvallon, 2004*

The time has come to give a brief account of the history of this "ism," to explain where and when it was coined, why it was given a negative meaning, and by whom, and why a political, not a moral, nature was attributed to it. The thinker responsible for showing individualism to be a "misguided judgment" and a defect of the citizen and not a quality of man as such was Tocqueville, who had also insisted on the fact that it was a modern and new concept, and one that was hard to understand for those who, like his French and European contemporaries, were not living in a society that was producing it naturally. If they confused it with egoism, it was for the following reason.

Although "individualism" is associated with Anglo-American culture and economic liberalism, the term was coined in France in a climate decidedly hostile to market society. Confirmation of this fact is provided by the first English translator of Tocqueville's *Democracy in America*, Henry Reeve, who apologized to his readers for having to use a Gallicism—individualism—to translate a word that did not have an English counterpart: "I know of no English word exactly equivalent to the expression."[1] The OED still uses this remark even today to confirm both the modernity of the term and, above all, the fact that it was not anglophone in origin.

The original connotation of the term was ideological and pejorative, as its French "inventors" were fully aware. Here is what Tocqueville wrote: " 'Individualism' is a word recently coined to express a new idea. Our fathers only knew about egoism. Egoism is a passionate and exaggerated love of self which leads a man to think of all things in terms of himself and to prefer himself to all. Individualism is a calm and considered feeling which disposes each citizen to isolate himself from the mass of his fellows and withdraw into the circle of family and friends; with this little society formed to his taste, he gladly leaves the greater society to look after itself."[2]

We shall return below to this important distinction between unbridled "love of self" (egoism) and a "calm and considered feeling" (individualism), between the frenzied desire to obtain the maximum for oneself and the silent withdrawal from society in order to seek tranquillity in private life. Let us now ponder another point highlighted by Tocqueville, a paradox that serves to furnish the meaning not only of modernity and of the complexities of the idea of individualism but also of the absolute originality of the society that spontaneously generates it, that is, democracy (in Tocqueville's day, the American form of it): the term had been coined in France to designate a condition that was nonetheless not yet familiar to the French, who in fact identified it with egoism. For their part, the Americans were individualists in practice but without showing themselves to be aware of it, if it is true that, wishing to give a name to their individualist condition, they were obliged to fall back upon a Gallicism, and a word that, moreover, had first been introduced with a pejorative intent.

The paradox captured very well the different attitudes of Europeans (the French in this case) and Americans toward modern society: "Of all the countries in the world, America is the one in which the precepts of Descartes are least studied and best followed."[3] In other words, in America moral and political ideas had been mental habits and practices of life before becoming philosophical doctrines. Like equality, individualism here lacked the radical and controversial connotations that might have clung to it had it first been theorized by philosophers and then been embraced by political leaders keen to impose it upon society in a Jacobin fashion. Through his American journey, Tocqueville had found confirmation of the fact that pragmatic reason was the best ally of social transformations, even the most radical ones, because it favored nonviolent processes of behavioral change, which allowed time for ideas and beliefs to settle. For this reason, he said, individualism was not as harmful in America as it was in France.

Insisting upon the modernity of individualism and the novelty of its American form, Tocqueville had anticipated a fact that was destined to become proverbial. Europeans would struggle to attain a correct understanding of it, because they could only call upon a conception that was freighted with negative meaning, as atomism and an antisocial disposition are. Individualism expressed first of all a fear, namely, that of seeing the world become a space inhabited by strangers, indifferent to the life and problems of society and without roots, each intent upon the exclusive satisfaction of her or his own interests. The communitarian antipathy toward difference, a response also found in our posttotalitarian societies, may be interpreted as a sign of a persisting tendency to think of individualism as negative in its effects upon social union. In actual fact, Tocqueville had observed that the Americans lived the individualist condition as positive, in part because their society was very far from lacking associative ties and was moreover structured by the two actual foundations of modern individualism: equality of conditions and of respect, and the politics of rights. Their society seemed to be the unplanned outcome of two forces that set out from, and returned to, the individual: a pronounced feeling of self-esteem and of proud dignity that found expression in the determination to look after one's own interests; an equally strong sense of responsibility toward the community, and even of patriotism. It was this mixture of self-assertion and of civic loyalty, of individual autonomy and social responsibility that had so impressed Tocqueville. In essence, individualism could be either an antisocial and disruptive force or an integrative force and a modern factor of unity. Two quotations may help to clarify this semantic divergence between the old and the new world over their respective ways of living and conceiving of individualism.

In 1843 a French "militant Catholic propagandist," Louis Veuillot, wrote the following lapidary words against individualism: "The evil which plagues France is not unknown; everyone agrees in giving it the same name: *individualism*. It is not difficult to see that a country where individualism reigns is no longer in the normal conditions of society, since society is the union of minds and interests, and individualism is division carried to the infinite degree. All for each, each for all, that is society; each for himself, and thus each against all, that is individualism." Two years earlier, in 1841, the anonymous reviewer of *Democracy in America* writing for a transcendentalist journal, the *Boston Quarterly Review*, had proposed a very different image: here individualism was a positive attitude toward life; it suggested the faith of individuals in themselves under the sway of "immutable laws," which, if unimpeded, "must in the end assimilate the species, and evolve all the glorious phenomena of original and eternal *order*;—that order which exists in man himself, and alone vivifies and sustains him."[4]

For the French Catholic author, individualism was to be equated with solipsism, conflict, erosion of the sense of duty, egoism, indifference toward the fate of others and the general good. Above all, it was a subversion of the hierarchical order, because the legitimacy of individual decisions was entrusted to individual judgment (subject therefore to such factors as pleasure, expediency, and opinion) rather than to external and higher authorities, repositories of the knowledge of the good and the just, such as the church and the state. Individualism was an acid liable to corrode both religious faith and the sense of the nation, because it accorded priority to rights and to individual conscience, depriving obedience of its absolute status. Even today conservatives, or those who exalt communities of belonging ("our land," "our people"), speak of individualism in just such negative terms.

Conversely, for the American Protestant author, individualism was an expression of moral autonomy and denoted free and responsible endeavor; it was not charged with fostering anarchy and atomism but valued for its capacity to stimulate the realization of a true union, not only between friends or the citizens of one and the same country, but with the whole of humanity and all Creation. Above all, individualism was at the origin of a sincerity of faith that had deeply impressed Tocqueville himself, since he was convinced, like John Locke, that only where there was religious liberty could faith be other than a hypocritical formalism and play a positive ethical role, for example, consolidating the sense of trust upon which voluntary human relationships, in the market or in politics, are built. If, as contemporary theorists of postsecularism maintain, the presence of religions in the public sphere not only does not undermine tolerance but is rather a force serving to regenerate the social values upon which the modern liberal state rests,[5] it should further be specified that this is possible precisely thanks to democracy. It is thanks to the "moral depth" of the culture of rights that religion can play this role.[6] This is because democratic society honors individualism and associates it with positive characteristics and forces: sincerity (hence the fine-tuning of institutions and rules ensuring transparency and checks upon the constituted authorities), responsibility (hence the equality of all citizens before the law), union with others (hence liberty of association), empathetic participation in the life of the nation and of humanity (hence the politics of social justice and national solidarity, the norms of hospitality and of political asylum for refugees from the entire world, the various forms of international humanitarian intervention).

The polysemy of the idea of individualism is rooted in its history. It is customary to attribute the original use of the term to Joseph de Maistre, the counterrevolutionary thinker and founder of modern reactionary thought. The word thus appeared in a private conversation of his which may be dated to 1820.[7] Yet the first to use it publicly were the Saint-Simonians, from the mid-1820s, in their review, *Le Producteur*, and above all Auguste Comte, the founder of philosophical positivism.[8] Both de Maistre and Comte bewailed the crisis of authority in modern society, a condition they saw as deriving from the Protestant Reformation: Luther's disobedience in the name of sincerity of faith had opened up an abyss in European society, shattering the ethical and religious concord of the whole continent and shifting its center of gravity from religious authority to individual conscience, a locus of sovereignty that exercised a fatal centripetal force. Protestantism was the first blow struck at transcendence, an important step along the path toward the human reappropriation of norms. According to de Maistre (and subsequently, Tocqueville, albeit without any counterrevolutionary intent), the outcome of the Reformation was ineluctably democracy, the absurd claim to base law and authority upon the principle of counting votes, and social union upon discordant opinions and preferences: "A time will come in which two friends, though having the same convictions and the same goal, will not understand each other at all."[9] This was why, according to this argument, rebellion against the Church of Rome and democracy were each the product of the other, the consequence of the individualistic force that had shattered the unity of the old Continent (one cannot help but notice here, with justified apprehension, how the leaders of the European Union have even today envisaged consolidating the tie between the different states using not only institutional factors but also the Christian religion, as the debate on mentioning God in the Union treaty demonstrates).

De Maistre and Comte held individualism morally responsible for a state of disorder that could be corrected only by the restoration of authority—of the authority of God in the one case and of scientific truth in the other. After the upheaval

of the Revolution of 1789, de Maistre thus suggested to the
sovereigns of Europe that they revert to the theological sources of power, to that divine foundation without which authority remained suspended from individual judgment, an unstable
and always precarious thing. Comte and the positivists, for their
part, called for the creation of a meritocratic elite of technicians,
a class consisting of those we would today call business manag-
ers, chosen for their organizational competence and for their
capacity to govern society as they would have run an industry,
that is to say, by deploying a functional and anti-individualist
rationality, geared to promoting the good of the whole and not
liberty. Religion in the one case and science in the other—or
two forms of truth that cannot countenance dissent save as
error that is unplanned and to be corrected—were the solutions
that these two antiliberal thinkers proposed for the modern ill
that had been diagnosed, namely, social and political conflict,
the sovereignty of individual judgment. In both cases, individualism was cast in a profoundly negative light; in as negative
a light, indeed, as democratic politics, the site, they held, of
provisional and debatable solutions. The enemies of individualism were therefore here suggesting something of the utmost
importance: the identification of individualism with democratic
politics. They were in complete agreement with Tocqueville's
diagnosis regarding the nature of individualism, construing it
as a mode of existence of democratic society and not as a
moral vice. To recapitulate, individualism is a category of political theology, no less than sovereignty is. De Maistre located
it within "political Protestantism taken to the most absolute
individualism."[10] "Political Protestantism" therefore signified
politics limited by individual rights; it was the germ of the
theory of popular sovereignty and, finally, the justification for
revolution. The step toward democracy would turn out to have

been short: the individualism of rights, de Maistre concluded, naturally fosters the feeling of equality, the quest for "an association of men without sovereignty," a voluntary association united not in the body of the sovereign but in the social spirit that operates as an immanent and divine force, ubiquitous and disseminated across all minds and laws (general will, pantheism, democracy: de Maistre and Tocqueville would prove to be in close proximity).[11]

It is as well, however, to specify that French publicists from the age of the Restoration were not the first to have denounced social disintegration and individualism. Indeed, the history of this polemical category does, strictly speaking, begin in the England of the latter half of the eighteenth century. Thus, in his "Speech on the Economical Reform" of 1780, Edmund Burke, a highly respected member of the British Parliament and subsequently an outspoken critic of the French Revolution, likens individuals to "shadows" that pass, while "the commonwealth is fixed and stable."[12] But he was concerned here with individuals such as they had been imagined by the "mechanistic philosophy" of the Continent, an abstract rationalism that, since Descartes, had led directly, according to Burke, to the Encyclopedists and the Jacobins; unconnected individuals whom the light of modern, utilitarian reason rendered more "savage and brutal" than the barbarians, because rapacious in pursuing their own interests and unrestrained in claiming their rights.[13] This individualism lay at the origin, in Burke's view, of the craze for assemblies and for democracy that had swept away the noble castes and the monarchy in France, nullifying traditions and rules shared through centuries of customs handed down from generation to generation. The Revolution and the guillotine were therefore the final but altogether logical outcome of an individualism proclaimed in the name not of a historical tradition but of reason and natural rights, and consequently serving as a weapon against every tradition and established authority, and one that would erase all historical and social differences. This individualism went hand in hand with equality: it was synonymous once again with democracy, the name of the worst political regime because it was the despotism of numbers, an aggregate of "sheep" united through the rhetoric of popular leaders that dragged them hither and thither and deceived them into supposing that they obeyed of their own free will.

By means of his trenchant critique of the individualism of natural rights, Burke implied that there could be, indeed, that there was another type of individualism, synonymous not with egoistic atomism but with a reasoned private wisdom, and an adherence to an order of values that rewarded individual responsibility while steering it toward social roles: family, profession, native land, political institutions; which nurtured the love of a form of civil liberty that had nothing to do with license and the natural instinct to possess, nor above all with the claiming of equal rights and democratic self-determination. The mild, innocuous individualism that the traditionalist Burke had in mind was the sort that had arisen as if naturally in England, in the shadow of tradition and the rights proclaimed in 1688, not in order to overturn the monarchy but to render it constitutional.

Burke's idea seemed to tally with the one inspiring the Puritans of New England, those whom Tocqueville would admire as citizens of a "good" democracy capable of differentiating between individualism as respect and militant egoism. In *Magnalia Christi Americana*, Cotton Mather, an influential eighteenth-century preacher, had interpreted the history of the American colonies as an example of the marvelous combination of the reformed religious spirit and individual sovereignty, of a sense of community and a proud independence of judgment. Mather sketched out a definition of liberty that some decades later Kant would put into philosophical language: "Nor would I have you to mistake in the point of your own *liberty*. There is a *liberty* of corrupt nature which is affected by *men* and *beasts* to do what they list; and this *liberty* is inconsistent with *authority*, impatient of all restraint; by this *liberty*, *Sumus Omnes Deteriores*, 'tis the grand enemy of *truth* and *peace*, and all the *ordinances* of God are bent against it. But there is a civil, a moral, a federal *liberty*, which is the proper end and object of *authority*; it is a *liberty* for that only which is *just* and *good*; for this *liberty* you are to stand with the hazard of your very *lives*."[14]

Liberty as the license to act outside the rules and liberty as the autonomous choice to do one's duty: in the former case individualism was certainly a dissolution of human solidarity and an expression of the tyranny of the individual's arbitrary will; in the latter case, it was the cement of social cooperation. Even French critics such as de Maistre and Comte might have endorsed this interpretation; save that for them the correction of "bad" individualism depended upon inverting the pyramid in order to return the individual to his position of subordination with regard to the good of the group and to whoever had the competence and authority to make decisions. Hence, if the critics of Enlightenment thought were able to reach a general consensus regarding egoistic and antisocial individualism, they parted company over the solutions to be adopted, since only the English and Americans reckoned that the answer lay in seeking in individual conscience the source of the norm of the good and of the just, a queen capable of ordering individual choices in such a way that they served to complement the social order. One author who was quite explicit about this difference was Thomas Carlyle, who overturned the framework of the French critics and came to the conclusion that not the Reformation but Catholicism had given birth to the Revolution of '89, because from hierarchy there could only come imposed and hypocritical obedience and the consequent spirit of rebellion and antisocial individualism, never a community of the just. For Carlyle, Luther had abolished the pope, not individual excellence—individualism, not individuality.[15]

In the mid-twentieth century, Friedrich von Hayek identified this individualism—by which I mean that of Burke or of Mather—with the character of a society capable of regulating itself.[16] As we shall see in the next chapter, the individuals of whom Hayek spoke in the 1940s were agents impelled to contribute to the social order not directly intending to do so but rather because they had been left at liberty to pursue their own interests; the sole provisos were that all were equally well-informed and that all owed obedience to a civil law whose legitimacy depended not upon the fact of it having been created by an act of collective will but upon the fact of it being the work of many generations bound together by a moral culture and consolidated juridical habits. "The freedom of the British which in the eighteenth century the rest of Europe came so much to admire was thus not, as the British themselves were among the first to believe and as Montesquieu later taught the world, originally a product of the separation of powers between legislature and the executive, but rather a result of the fact that the law that governed the decisions of the courts was the common law, a law existing independently of anyone's will and at the same time binding upon and developed by the independent courts; a law with which parliament only rarely interfered and, when it did, mainly only to clear up doubtful points within a given body of law. One might even say that a sort of separation of powers had grown up in England, not because the 'legislature' alone made law, but because it did *not:* because the law was determined by courts independent of the power which organized and directed government, the power namely of what was misleadingly called the 'legislature.' "[17]

The antidemocratic conservative Burke and the individualist liberal Hayek were agreed on one highly important point: the social order has within itself the foundations of its own legitimacy; the role of politics is to respect and protect these foundations, not to subvert them or to seek to mold them to an idea of the just society. The difference between the two was that whereas Burke argued from the viewpoint of a historical tradition articulated through orders and castes (just as the England of his own day was), Hayek thought of the social order in terms of the self-regulating force of individual interests and of the distribution of merits and honors through the market. This was not a trifling difference, but neither was it so great as to prevent these two forms of conservatism—one based upon caste tradition and the other upon the market—being allied in the struggle against the common enemy: the philosophies which assign centrality to the political will and to the demand for legitimacy; which propose to mold and reform society, either to promote more justice or to create more equality, but in either case to attain objectives associated human beings neither do nor can produce spontaneously and naturally. The alliance that in contemporary Italy has evidently been sealed between traditionalist and free market conceptions, between an identitarian or religious communitarianism and economic liberalism, and against social democratic or social-liberal visions, is descended from this conception of society and politics, which in its own fashion is antiegalitarian and critical of Enlightenment public reason.

However, the "true" individualism to which Hayek appealed when criticizing the democratic individualism of French origin was not the kind born of the civic piety of the Puritans but rather that motivated by commercial prudence and the calculation of interests. Or, to put it more precisely, Hayek retrieved and extolled only one of the two aspects of which it consisted: not the republican "ardor" for the public good (of central importance to the American founding fathers, who had after all been brought up in the Calvinist faith, which has a republican foundation) but the "ardor" for the attainment of affluence and a determination to rely only on one's own strength. More than to the sermons of the Reverend Dr. Mather or to the speeches of the conservative Burke, it would be appropriate to link the thought of Hayek to the current of thought that looks to *The Fable of the Bees* by Bernard de Mandeville, a book which, like *The Prince* of Machiavelli, declared its intention to represent men "as they really are" and not "as they ought to be" and which, after having denounced the hypocrisy with which individuals mask their true intentions, showed how the human vices most roundly castigated by religion and ordinary morality were in reality the certain source of the civic virtues, so long as men were left free to follow their own course. Individual interest was the friend of general interest, but only on condition that this latter was not pursued intentionally. "Great Wealth and Foreign Treasure will ever seem to come among Men, unless you'll admit their inseparable Companions, Avarice and Luxury."[18] The rule holding everything together was that of the heterogeneity of ends or the argument of unintended consequences, a surrogate for the invisible hand that led each to contribute to the general interest, not because they were striving to act virtuously but because they were consistently pursuing their own interests without any trickery.

If all acted rationally in pursuit of their own advantage and without using the market as a casino (that is, without cheating), the entire society would gain thereby. As Adam Smith had already written in *The Wealth of Nations:* "It is not from the benevolence of the butcher, the brewer, or the baker, that we expect our dinner, but from their regard to their own interest."[19] Furthermore, Jon Elster has explained, striving to be virtuous by sheer will and by imposing virtue upon oneself is not only an unfeasible task to undertake consistently and in the long run but also very much a minority pursuit. An argument built upon reasons and justifications can be reproduced at will at any moment; the same is not true of a feeling, which is not so mechanical and needs to be stimulated and cultivated in order to take shape and resist over time.[20] But individual interests may induce the greater number to do spontaneously whatever has an appropriate rationality. For this reason, if society was so organized that it rewarded individual enterprise, all would profit from the egoism of each, while liberty would send down firm roots into the passions and into the reason of individuals, without there being any need for it to be buttressed by virtue and duty. It is not the appeal to solidarity that will convince individuals to do what would be in the common interest and consequently to temper their own passions but rather the personal experience that reining in those passions furthers the aim of increasing their own personal advantage.

This spontaneous relationship between self-repression and individual interest is at the basis of what is the most useful sentiment, the cement of modern society, namely, trust. There is no need to devise institutional mechanisms or to punish with the law in order to instill a spirit of cooperation and solidarity in individuals reluctant to do good; it is enough to act indirectly upon their most natural emotions and to let reward and punishment follow the self-interested conduct of the individual. For, as David Hume observed of these same sentiments: "As their merit consists in their tendency to serve the person, possessed of them, without any magnificent claim to public and social desert, we are the less jealous of their pretensions, and readily admit them into the catalogue of laudable qualities. We are not sensible that, by this concession, we have paved the way for all the other moral excellencies, and cannot consistently hesitate any longer, with regard to disinterested benevolence, patriotism, and humanity."[21]

However, just like the virtuous citizen of New England, the wise and industrious egoist depicted by Smith and Mandeville was as far as can be from the image of an individual who is asocial, dissociated, anarchic, or, to use Burke's term, unconnected. An individual of that ilk presupposed a structured society, a solid ethical culture and good laws if he were to succeed in pursuing his own egoistic plans; besides, he needed everyone to share the same fundamental values, to be motivated by the same interest, to have access to the same information, and, above all, to be able to trust one another. Individualism presupposed that all respected contracts, that they played fairly, and by the same rules, that in short they had a normative community to refer to, a common sense that united society and effortlessly directed the individual will. It presupposed an ordered society, one that was not violent but also not encased in values or traditions that might impede the action of individuals in an irrational fashion so far as economic prudence was concerned. Finally, it presupposed a community of persons who accorded each other recognition, who spoke, as it were, the same ethical language, who were imbued with the same mores. Once again there comes to light the close relationship, which is not one of opposition, between individualism and ethical community.

As we shall shortly see, in the Cold War years, when the ideological struggle between market society and collectivist society assumed the guise of a quasi-religious struggle between liberty and slavery, the meaning of individualism ceased to be what it had been in the nineteenth century and acquired indubitably positive characteristics. Individualism was propounded as the pivotal doctrine of liberalism and ultimately as a synonym of civilization against barbarism, of the ethos of free competition against communism and the planned economy. That ideological battle sought its foundations in history. Indeed, it created them in an altogether fantastical manner, imagining that the genesis of individualism lay in the struggle against collectivism and socialism. It is worth devoting a few words to this ideological interpretation of history.

Léo Moulin, a follower of Hayek though less brilliant and not so well known, maintained in an essay from 1955 that the term "socialism" was introduced into the political lexicon after 1830 as a response to individualism. According to Moulin, the opposition between individualists and anti-individualists arose out of the contrast between two models of society, one liberal and the other socialist: between antistatism and statism. In order to prove his thesis, Moulin dug out the *Discourses* of Pierre Leroux (written between 1831 and 1832), a critic of the Orleanist revolution who set out to unmask the "betrayers" of the principles of '89, that is, the supporters of the individualist ideology.[22] Leroux's indictment was directed against the laissez-faire doctrinaires, because they had demanded political rights exclusively for property owners, the new oligarchy of post-Napoleonic France, the industrial and financial caste that had supplanted the nobles of the ancien régime. The republican Leroux criticized individualism for two reasons, both of them political: first, because it denied republican fraternity; and second, because, by linking voting rights to fiscal contributions and to property, it violated political equality. Citizenship had become an explicit instrument for the defense of economic interests, as Karl Marx himself would shortly come to argue.

In contrast to the interpretation later advanced by the Hayekian Moulin, Leroux thus maintained that the individualists were enemies of the republican idea of sovereignty more than of socialism; they were enemies of the general good because they had extended the egoistic principle from the economic to the political sphere. The origin of the attack upon individualism was therefore to be sought primarily not in socialist ideology but in republican patriotism.

Leroux's critique brought to light a very important, and still highly current, problem: liberal hegemony had shattered the link between individual liberty and equality established by the Revolution of '89. Along with this link, the identity between the individual and the citizen, and between civil and political rights, was likewise being shattered. The consequence was that civil rights were interpreted in a fashion that we would today term neoliberal, that is, as rights of the individual "against" the state, disassociated from responsibility toward the political community. One may thus readily understand the hostility of the republican Leroux: "It is individualism that they [the liberals] are defending; it is egoism that they are protecting." In short, individualism appeared to be the ideological weapon used by the supporters of laissez-faire liberalism to ferry egoism and competition from the moral and economic to the political sphere. It had enabled the economic liberals to shatter the political tie between one and all in order to accord preeminence to the first of the two factors: individualism "expresses in law the sovereignty of each!"[23]

It is interesting to note that Leroux attacked individualism in the section of his book that was devoted to the foundations of sovereignty. He therefore imputed to individualism a political meaning that was no longer the same as egoism, thus anticipating the distinction soon to be clarified by Tocqueville. Individualism was an ideology of the citizen in his dealings with the state or, as I explained above, the index of a conception of politics as an instrument for the advancement of private ends.

What emerges from this cursory analysis of a now all but forgotten work by Leroux is that, contrary to the ideological interpretation of the Hayekian liberals, the first attack upon individualism came not from socialism but from republicanism. The first radical alternative brought to light by modern society, as Constant and Arendt had stressed, was that between political virtue (the public good) and individual interests or private good (individualism)—an alternative that became the ideological fulcrum not only of traditionalists and conservatives like Burke but also of republican thinkers, in other words, of all those who set great store by political authority.

This clarification permits a further reference to contemporary political theory, inasmuch as the critiques of individualism also feature precisely the accusation that it has corroded the sense of community, without which society is nothing else but a battlefield pitting antagonistic interests one against the other. The rebirth of communitarianism in the years of Reaganite and Thatcherite hegemony confirms this interpretation. A few years ago Alasdair MacIntyre argued that national political identity has a tendency to go missing, because the idea of a nonrational good such as the love of one's own land is alien to the logic of self-interest: the patriotism of those who put rights before duties is nothing else but a utilitarian gratitude. Individualism in this case prefigures a society in which the rulers neither denote nor represent the "moral community" but are merely a set of institutions and procedures peculiar to a bureaucratic state, the sustaining of which requires not an affective or ethical consensus but simply an agreement of a commercial kind, as though it were a cost to be paid for a benefit enjoyed.[24]

In a volume with the revealing title *La paura e la speranza* (Fear and hope) published in 2008, the then minister of finance in Berlusconi's cabinet, Mr. Giulio Tremonti, rediscovered some of these old concepts, corroborating a century and a half later the interpretation proposed by Leroux, to the effect that individualism's great adversary, before and more than socialism, has been (and is) an identitary vision of the community, whether it is called family, religion, nation, or region: a common good without which the individual may become an anarchical element. The community comes to the rescue—according to this vision—not so as to substitute itself for the individual but in order to overcome the anomic individualism fostered by the bureaucratic state dispensing services and social justice. No sooner has the welfare state depersonalized the individual than it destroys the communities of choice. But community and individual may reestablish a sort of coherent and harmonious relationship if the former substitutes itself for the state in the management and distribution of the functions of solidarity, and if the latter plays its own role as economic actor pursuing its own advantage. From the redistributive logic characteristic of a bureaucratic "cold rationality" one proceeds in this way to communitarian solidarity.[25] Individualism is here a name designating a society lacking a center, composed of disassociated individuals, and lacking an order of values and an authority higher than that of the individual conscience: above all, it is identified with a politics founded upon equality, and one that does not hesitate to resort to public intervention in order to remove the obstacles that lie in its path, a politics that is open and tolerant of differences, and one whose purpose is not to defend the cultural identity of the group.

The conservative liberalism of our own time arose within democratic society as a gemmation of economic liberalism; it has manifested itself as a reaction to the disillusionment with planned society in the postwar period and as a rediscovery of communities in the guise of surrogates for state welfare programs; a functional response, in other words, to a society that remains unrepentantly modeled upon business and laissez-faire. Analyzed as an ideological phenomenon, conservative liberalism derived from critical reflection upon "expectations-gone-wrong," to revive one of Albert Hirschman's most felicitous notions. Hirschman, in his reconstruction of the cycles of enthusiasm and disillusion evident in the history of the private/public dichotomy and of the reactions to it, has argued that an important phase of Western civilization has been marked precisely by the intellectual atmosphere inspired by the feeling of dissatisfaction associated with economic individualism: unhappiness and dissatisfaction with "insatiability" and the unceasing quest for the gratification of needs, which, while they may keep society in motion, induce individuals to reflect critically upon the value of material wealth and therefore also on models and styles of life, and finally on the idea of the good society.[26] In the light of Hirschman's suggestion, I would argue that taking seriously the disillusion/enthusiasm alternation that has accompanied individualism is a useful perspective from which to analyze critically the role of the state in modern democracy.

V

The Individual against Politics

Man in any complex society can have no choice but between adjusting himself to what to him must seem the blind forces of the social process and obeying the orders of a superior. So long as he knows only the hard discipline of the market, he may well think the direction by some other intelligent human brain preferable; but, when he tries it, he soon discovers that the former still leaves him at least some choice, while the latter leaves him none, and that it is better to have a choice between unpleasant alternatives than being coerced into one.

—*Friedrich A. von Hayek, 1949*

I n every generation freedom is threatened by those who regard the individual person as inferior to some supposed collective whole . . . the intellectual battle between the individualist and the collectivist is never won, but it remains important to fight it."[1] This battle is inflected in different ways, as the polemical objectives alter. As we have seen, in the first half of the nineteenth century, individualism was in the dock. Conversely, in our own day, society has been indicted, and in the name of individualism. In the present chapter we shall be concerned with this more recent battle, that is to say, with the redefinition, in an antistatist sense, of freedom accompanying the democratization of the postwar period, within the international framework of the Cold War and of the ideological clash between the liberal and communist models.[2] If when individualism made its first appearance in a Europe lit up by hopes of national rebirth it was thrown on to the defensive, with the readjustment of the industrial economy and of government limited to the defense of individual rights, it has since then been portrayed as an expression of moral and civil progress and, above all, of freedom.

The rehabilitation of individualism began, however, in England, at the end of the nineteenth century, alongside the imperial self-congratulation so all-pervasive during the latter half of the reign of Queen Victoria.[3] The expansion of the British Commonwealth had defeated the resistance put up by the social liberalism of Mill to the "old economic school" of the free market, and legitimized an unmitigated glorification of individualism. Herbert Spencer was the popularizer who embodied this ideological reversal; he was the first philosopher to employ the doctrine of laissez-faire as a sociological rule to explain the free society and moral progress, two conditions that, in his view, could advance in tandem only to the extent that government intervention was limited to the essential security functions, allowing society to follow the blueprint marked out by the interests and the preferences of individuals. Individualism coincided with, and was identified with, an extraordinary reaction of civil society against politics and the state. This was the meaning of the moral maxim of self-help popularized by Samuel Smiles, "Heaven helps those that help themselves" (a maxim that is timeless, if it is true that the corresponding myth of the self-made man has dominated Italian political life for the past two decades), the transformation of which into mental habit and custom was supposed, according to the expectations of the economists and the moralists, to defeat poverty and render each person fully responsible for her or his own fate.[4] Spencer himself defended his doctrine of progress by raising the alarming specter of a collectivist society in which the central planning of the economy and of social life would have rendered all persons not only less free but also less responsible toward themselves, their own families, and, finally, the nation and humanity.[5]

Social Darwinism was the name of this doctrine, which equated justice with the social competition in which all were supposed to participate and which alone was capable, through its objective and impartial criteria, of proclaiming the victors and the vanquished. These latter, the poor, were deemed to be responsible for their own failure and were seen as the inevitable dead wood in what today we would call a "risk" society that no one in particular could be expected to direct. The losers could hope for nothing more than the charity of the victors. The phenomenology of the charitable act, which Emerson describes in much the same way as the young Marx, assumes the form, so far as the perpetrator is concerned, of seeking to justify one's existence in the world by the paying of a fee for the mere fact of being a sinner. Its foundation is the religious phenomenon of repentance. Charity, as Emerson sarcastically observed only a few years prior to Spencer's texts, is an act of ambition in the perpetrator whereby he seeks to be purified for what to his conscience appears far from noble; however, it ennobles neither the donor nor the object of charity. The donor is not ennobled, because the motivation behind her giving is instrumental; it is the salvation of her soul, or, in a secularized perspective, the approval and esteem of others; nor is the object of charity ennobled, because beneficence creates dependents and is a powerful means of conserving the social order, which, while it throws a lifebelt to the luckless and enables them to enjoy vicariously the wealth of others, eases the conscience of the victors in the social competition, putting them at peace with themselves where the social costs of their prosperity are concerned, and reassuring them that they have done their duty through having given the best possible expression to the talents they have received from the Creator.[6] Social Darwinism, with the moralistic appendix of charity, has functioned as a secularization of Calvinist ethics, the ethical kernel and the inner, regenerative core of a constantly revitalized capitalism.

In opposition to social Darwinism, and precisely when the British Empire was at its height, anti-Spencerian liberals (also called "neo-idealists") such as Thomas H. Green and Leonard T. Hobhouse attempted a no less interesting procedure, one destined to have a long future: they salvaged individualism in the context of an ethical vision of a just and liberal society. By contrast with Spencer, these idealists saw in individualism the sign of a society that rightly placed human nature first and made the person the ultimate goal of social well-being, a goal that did, however, require competent action on the part of government, and not an abstention from politics. Interventions involving redistributive justice, succoring need, but also championing the right to work, the activation of social services, and the building of a public education system were theorized (and after the First World War concretely implemented by the British state and by local authorities) as strategies promoting a liberal society conducive to the fulfillment of the individual. To Green and Hobhouse, the distance between liberalism and socialism therefore did not seem to be so very great; it was if anything the consequence more of doctrinaire and ideological differences than of empirical questions or of issues of social prudence. These liberals "were not militantly egalitarian because they thought that *poverty and dependency* were more pressing problems than economic inequality itself."[7]

The openness of individualism to social justice had already been argued by the father of pragmatist philosophy, Charles Sanders Peirce, who in 1893 had written sarcastically that the political economy of the nineteenth century had sought moral redemption by bending the Gospel to its need for accumulation: the conviction put about by the followers of Mandeville was that "private vices of every kind are public benefits," and that an individual, by crushing his neighbor, does right by them both. Except for the fact that, as the "sentimental" Peirce commented, this "gospel of greed" is entirely at odds with the Sermon on the Mount, in which Jesus (like Socrates) exhorted his listeners to contravene codified morality for the sake of their own self-respect. "So a miser is a beneficent power in a community, is he? With the same reason precisely, only in a much higher degree, you might pronounce the Wall Street sharp to be a good angel, who takes money from heedless persons not likely to guard it properly, who wrecks feeble enterprises better stopped, and who administers wholesome lessons to unwary scientific men, by passing worthless checks upon them,—as you did, the other day, to me, my millionaire Master in glomery, when you thought you saw your way."[8] Likewise at odds with the "possessive" I was democratic individualism, which, being based both upon faith in oneself and upon sympathetic communication with others, had a disposition that was neither centripetal nor accumulative. "When I spoke or speak of the democratic element—Emerson noted in his diary—I do not mean that ill thing vain and loud which writes lying newspapers, spouts at caucuses, and sells its lies for gold, but that spirit of love for the General good whose name this assumes."[9]

Yet of the two currents of social thought well disposed toward individualism, the one represented by Spencer was indubitably the progenitor of the economic liberalism that found favor after the Second World War. From the political point of view, the reaction against the totalitarianisms was a reaction against the politics of economic planning and statism; from the philosophical point of view, the liberal revival coincided with a reappropriation of individualism affecting the social and political sciences no less than political philosophy. Admittedly, liberal individualism was not the only protagonist of this revival; Christian personalism and secular existentialism were just as important in the shaping of posttotalitarian Europe. But the contrast between liberty and collectivism was more coherently pointed up by economic individualism. The Austrian school played a crucial role in this regard, not least because of its influence in transforming American political science in the aftermath of the Second World War. In America and in England, "individualism" in those years became the name of a system of thought that was at once descriptive and prescriptive.

Methodological individualism, as this antiholistic doctrine of sociological explanation was called, was presented as being equidistant from the utopias of the left and those of the right,

from communist collectivisms and fascist statisms, all doctrinaire forms held to subordinate the task of theoretical analysis
to a model of the good society to be realized. Against these
pseudo-scientific aberrations, methodological individualism
prided itself upon being the objective response to all the ideologies. To Ludwig von Mises the critics of individualism were
the enemies of liberty and of the market economy, while Hayek,
for his part, distinguished between two different visions of
individualism, only one of which in his judgment merited the
epithet "true."[10] "False" individualism was the kind cultivated
by all the political philosophies of romantic origin, but especially those of a Marxist matrix, which were held to engender
two fundamental vices: first, the identification of individual
liberty with the realization of a perfect autonomy and hence
the justification of social policies geared to freeing individuals
from need; and, second, the foundation of these policies upon
presumed scientific laws of society and of history, but in actual fact a product of abstract and unfalsifiable visions, and
therefore readily turned into a dogmatic faith. "False" individualism was, finally, the kind that, in the name of the achieve-
ment of individual well-being and of a therapeutic vision of
justice, mobilized bureaucratic "cold rationality," burying, together with individual responsibility, the possibility that capitalism offers each person of being the "author of their own good
fortune."[11]

At the origin of methodological individualism there was
the proposal to counterpose to the abstract and rationalistic
"science" of Continental philosophies of history a "theory" of
society that set out to show how it was that social forces were
simply the outcome of individual choices and actions. As Karl
Popper came to write, "All social phenomena, and especially
the functioning of all social institutions, should always be

understood as resulting from the decisions, actions, attitudes, etc., of human individuals"; and, he added, "we should never be satisfied by an explanation in terms of so-called 'collective' [actors]."[12] Liberty could not be engineered but would emerge spontaneously, so long as individuals were allowed to pursue their own preferences and interests. It was not through an act of political will or by the decisions of central committees or parliamentary assemblies that a free and just society would be consolidated but through the unpremeditated coordination of individual actions. The unanticipated virtuous effects produced by individual agents may be explained by the regularity of behavior, by the fact that all act in response to the same inputs; these effects issue from individual interest. Hobbes was the first and most authoritative theorist of methodological individualism, by dint of an analysis that proposes to relate conduct to its objective and constitutive causes: fear and rational calculation as a response to fear.

Be this as it may, the introducing of a nonanalytic causality, as when "class" and "nation" and even "society" are brought into play, as if collective persons or entities preexisting the relations between individuals were involved, was for these individualist liberals as ideological as speaking of "social justice" or of any "ought to be" that artificially dignifies actual existence, the economic behavior of individuals, and their personal motivations. These holistic perspectives, and it mattered not at all to such thinkers whether they were tied to revolutionary explanations such as Marxism or to reformist sophistries such as liberal and democratic socialism, presupposed a "personification of society," and treated society as a living organism in which individuals and their freedom of choice featured as functions subordinated to the good of all and rational only inasmuch as they were directed by a government or by a central motor of

planning that coordinated them in terms of a goal that a political will decreed to be rational and just. In this organicist and
systemic vision, Hayek wrote, individuals lose specific value and
become functional means to an end that transcends them all
and that supposes itself to be superior to each of them. In
conclusion: every conception of society that violated this individualistic interpretation—an interpretation dubbed methodological but in reality ideological precisely on account of
the oppositional and polemical character that distinguished
it—appeared to be a form of collectivism from which individual liberty was completely absent. The "road to serfdom" was in
reality the road to politics, the legacy of the Enlightenment
utopia of using the law and institutions as instruments to resolve
social contradictions and to create a harmony of interests.[13]

The premise of this liberal (and free-market) critique was
that the individual, an actor of a unique value and one that was
above all uniform in his motivations, could be respected only
in a society that entertained just the one sort of liberty, the
negative one; a society that did not steer behaviors toward
cooperation but left them free to satisfy "appetites" as best they
might, according to the eighteenth-century maxim formulated
by David Hume: it is not the appeal to the general good that
will convince individuals to direct their natural passions toward
social goals but rather the possibility of freely expressing those
passions, since from that liberty, and without premeditation,
social good will issue. Once single individuals had been recognized as the motors of history and of society, every conception
that assigned to "structure" or to "functions" rational capacities
for choice or causal determination led fatally to a preordaining
of the fate of persons by impairing their liberty of choice, the
only liberty worthy of the name, and finally compromising
social well-being itself. There is liberty, Isaiah Berlin wrote in

1958, only and insofar as interferences with the actions of the individual do not occur. One does not need to know the nature of such interferences in order to conclude that their presence obstructs liberty: every discourse designed to define the nature of the interference strays fatally from the analytico-conceptual dimension (what liberty is) to the normative dimension or to that of legitimacy (how liberty ought to be). But as Hobbes had declared in *Leviathan*, from the point of view of those who must obey the laws, or of those who suffer interference from the state in their choices, there is no difference, whether the laws are those of a republic or of an autocratic government. Be this as it may, anyone who does not obey them is punished. "Every law"—wrote Berlin, citing Jeremy Bentham—"is an infraction of liberty," and this maxim is valid for every regime, and, crucially, applies to all equally, as much to those who behave rationally as to those who behave irrationally. But "freedom is not freedom to do what is . . . wrong."[14] Every value judgment as to form of government therefore does nothing to alter the "fact" that where there is an obstacle—and the law is an obstacle—individual liberty is interrupted. We certainly are concerned with a functional interruption inasmuch as it enables individuals motivated by conflicting interests to live together peacefully; but the consequences (utility) do not alter the facts of the case. To quote Berlin once again, individual liberty may be enjoyed (or trampled upon) as much in an autocracy as in a democracy, and although "self-government may, on the whole, provide a better guarantee of the preservation of civil liberties," yet "there is no necessary connection between individual liberty and democratic rule."[15]

The fortune of methodological individualism has been surprising, and so successful has it been that it has even affected theorists adopting something bordering upon a socialist

stance, who have used neoclassical economics' critique of Marxism to emancipate this latter from the myth of "class," a metaphysical residue of an idea of a collective subject and actor in
history that is peculiar to a "positive" interpretation of liberty
as autonomy and liberation from alienation.[16] Recent experimental findings have brought out the ideological dimension of
this individualism and shown that individuals "display an attitude that is cooperative and characterized by mutual trust
even in contexts from which the effects of reputation are excluded," and even in contexts characterized by "anonymity," or
in ones that do not feature the anticipated and feared opinion
of others, the only natural deterrent admitted by the theorists
of economic individualism. Finally, the kind of conduct observed in these experiments "suggest[s] the hypothesis of *homo
oeconomicus*, whose behavior is entirely driven by the pursuit
of the maximum material advantage, a hypothesis that is not
borne out by reality, and that should therefore be used with
caution."[17]

The impact of methodological individualism most rele-
vant to the present book is the one that has permeated liberalism (above all, but not only economic liberalism) in the years
of postwar reconstruction and that had its heyday in the 1980s,
first in Great Britain and then in the United States, where it won
over governments and, with the triumph of neoliberalism,
unleashed an unmitigated laissez-faire revolution. Ironically
enough, we are concerned here with a revolution whose pro-
tagonists were in fact the governments, and which was directed
and implemented in a "Jacobin" fashion by means of centralized
"plans" for deregulation and liberalization, with a view to undermining not only the politics of redistribution and social
justice but also the practice of (trade union) collective bargain-
ing, the social security and labor legislation that had been

consolidated in the years of expansion of social rights, which I summarized in chapter 1 as the short-term history of the political culture of equal dignity. Contemporary economists have described this liberalization in terms of a putative "trickle-down" effect, whereby drops of wealth are supposed to percolate down to the entire society as a consequence of a general relaxation of the tax regime, which, while it greatly benefits the few, offers some relief to the many also, if for no other reason than because it stimulates production and gives everyone the sense of being relieved of a weight, or of a fiscal burden. The maxim "Heaven helps those who help themselves" thus supersedes social solidarity, a blanket that fiscal reduction has by now rendered all too threadbare. However, it has also led to the erosion of equal citizenship.

The ideal guiding this laissez-faire planning was the creation of a completely individualistic society in which the distribution of costs and of sacrifices would have been just precisely because and inasmuch as it had followed the paths of individual preferences, leaving it to the market to assess merit and need. The democratic societies in which we live today are set in this antipolitical utopia, which in its turn revolves around the entirely unproven idea that the force sanctioning selfish interests is sufficient, and that true sovereignty resides in the economic sphere. The outcomes of this utopia are, however, not reassuring, either on the economic plane or, and this is what concerns us here, in relation to the ideal of a society in which respect for persons follows naturally and directly from the exercise of liberty as noninterference, if no vision of the just society informs the actions of individuals.

We can at this point return to Hayek and to his conception of "true" individualism: "true" inasmuch as it is based upon an instrumental vision of politics regarding the interests and the

choices of individuals; "true" inasmuch as it is a negation of
every "conception" of "social justice." As in the classical liberal
tradition, by which I mean the one having its origin in John
Locke, government and the normative organization of public
life are justifiable inasmuch as they are functions in the service
of a higher and preexisting end: the defense of the property,
life, and liberty of individuals. The person, thus her/his basic
rights, is a nonnegotiable good and moreover a good in relation
to which a government's legitimacy is judged.

Politics is strictly speaking the coercive ordering of the
state, and as such an expedient artificially created (by contrast
with natural rights, which individuals do not create but recognize) by human beings on account of their failed attempt to
order their relations through consent alone, and without coercion. As Locke has explained in the *Second Treatise on Government*, in general self-government without coercion is within the
bounds of human possibility, but one cannot be certain of putting it into practice because inevitably there are individuals, even
if only a few, who violate natural rights, and who function by
departing from natural rationality. Original sin is an indication
of human frailty and imperfection, but also of the rationality,
although not of the feasibility, of the desire to live with others
as equals, without having to obey anyone else, only one's own
upright conscience. A desire that is impossible fully to satisfy,
for various reasons, such as ill-directed emotions or a lack of
information, shortcomings that a good education of the feelings
(effected in the primary natural societies such as the family and
the workplace) should successfully hold in check. Whatever the
cause of the harm may be, a small minority of deviants is sufficient to render coercion necessary. From this necessity the task
of government and of politics ineluctably follows: to guarantee
physical safety and the defense of fundamental rights through

the removal of the obstacles that prevent all individuals operating according to their own choices and guided by their own natural reasonableness. "The *State of Nature* has a Law of Nature to govern it, which obliges every one: And Reason, which is that Law, teaches all Mankind, who will but consult it, that being all equal and independent, no one ought to harm another in his Life, Health, Liberty, or Possessions. . . . In transgressing the Law of Nature, the Offender declares himself to live by another Rule, than that of *reason* and common Equity . . . and so he becomes dangerous to Mankind, the tye, which is to secure them from injury and violence, being slighted and broken by him. . . . I easily grant, that *Civil Government* is the proper Remedy for the Inconveniences of the State of Nature, which must certainly be Great, where Men may be Judges in their own Case."[18]

The central task of the liberal state is thus to repress, and in reality it is its reason for existing. Indeed, in the judgment of the free-market liberals, it is a task that ought not to be bolstered by others if the state is to stand any chance of being effective: for example, the task of redistributing wealth through taxation and hence of interpreting equality as something more than the equal opportunity to express one's own talents (civil rights). Every act of centralized planning would end up interfering regularly and systematically with individual choices, thereby artificially throwing natural rationality out of joint. In the end, this ambition to engineer things will engender not only artificial injustice but also an escalation of interferences through the law and hence less liberty in an absolute sense. A state that seeks to render society just inevitably ends up by being liberticidal, precisely because it betrays the task for which it has been constructed, namely, to guarantee the free fulfillment of individual choices by defending the liberty to own property and to exchange, the liberty to choose to believe in a god, and the liberty to associate with others; the liberty, in essence, to function in harmony with one's own individual conscience, while respecting the liberty of others. In order for it to perform this task, the only one legitimized by the consent of individuals to subject themselves to the command of the civil law, the state must be built according to very precise rules: limited in its functions; monitored by those who obey the law and not by those who make it; and, finally, subject to the electoral judgment of citizens. A liberal government is a limited government based upon consent, in which the judiciary plays a central role.

The supremacy of the judiciary in the liberal state is consistent with the theory that views politics as a means to coordinate in an indirect fashion the positive actions of individuals (commercial ventures, transactions, and associations entered into for any reason that is not illicit), to correct errors that individuals make in good faith (for example, for lack of sound information), or to suppress malevolent violations of natural and civil law. A state of this kind, Bobbio observed, derived from "an arbitrary reduction of all public law to penal law (which gives rise to the image of the night-watchman state)."[19]

This was the minimal state liberals such as Spencer and Hayek had in mind; a state in the service of a society which was free insofar as it was capable of regulating itself with the minimum expenditure of coercive power, but whose coercive power did nonetheless function effectively, was not used at the discretion of the powerful, and followed procedures that were impersonal and governed by precise rules.

In this interpretation of liberalism, individualism is thus not only an ideology (as a matter of fact, the methodological individualists categorically refused to be defined as ideological and insisted that if a lack of rationality and objectivity existed anywhere it was in the ranks of their fiercest opponents, the advocates of what they termed "false" individualism) but also a method by means of which individuals coordinate their actions and their lives in reciprocal relationships of self-interest and according to norms that, as we have seen, do not need will in order to be justified and imposed. In an entirely individualistic and liberal society, the sites and procedures of justice (the courts and the tribunals), rather than the will of a parliamentary assembly or of the executive arm of government, are the locus in which liberty is protected.

The theory of society as an order in which actions coordinate themselves by means of an instrumental reason that is universal is anchored to a negative conception of liberty, in which, as we have seen, the premise is that each of us knows what is good in itself and does not need to be directed by a authority that is external, let alone political, which would in any case be subject to the pressure of opinions (very often irrational, passionate, and prejudiced) or of numerical majorities (if one were dealing with a society with a democratic system). Social policies are strewn with mistaken interventions and corrupt actions, phenomena that are incentivized precisely by the sheer quantity of resources extorted from citizens by fiscal means. Proposals to enhance the flourishing of individuals or of capacities, a conception of politics as emancipation or justice, are at best actions that disrupt the order of the market and are, it is argued, unjustified limitations upon the liberty of individuals, where there is no certainty of benefiting them or of furthering their interests; at worst they are ideological factories in the service of kleptocracies that are completely out of control.[20]

A system of abstract rules and procedures, a law that is not retroactive, an impartial application of the norm—in essence, a political society in which politics is minimal and the

juridical order is highly structured—are the salient features of
the liberal state construed as a minimal state and founded upon
an individualistic vision of society. As may readily be intuited,
to create such a state is far from easy or to be taken for granted,
and, above all, far from natural, but sustained instead by an
ethos of individual responsibility and by a capacity for self-
sanctioning that is the expression of a specific ethico-religious
tradition; indeed, the expression, as Burke had clearly seen, of
a civil culture consolidated over the centuries and not one that
could be improvised or exported at will. The more recent utopia of the free-market individualists has strayed beyond the
bounds of tradition and has propounded the argument that,
the logic of interests and preferences being everywhere the same,
there is not or ought not to be any historical or contextual
limit to this model of society. The Iraqi adventure, conceived
and led by followers of the Hayekian school with a view to
pursuing the utopia of the recreation of the state of nature and
with it of liberal civil society, has been the Jacobin expression
of this utopia of neoliberal experimentalism. The problems that
stem from this antipolitical conception of individualism are
twofold. The first concerns respect for the dignity of the individual; the second has to do with the character of the individualist society. So far as the first problem is concerned, this
individualism is based upon an unproven assumption, and one
that is assumed to be unproblematic, although it is not: that
there is a spontaneous correlation between the fact that individuals have been left free to choose and to act in all that per-
sonally concerns them without suffering any interference, and
the fact that individuals respect one another as creatures possessed of equal dignity. Yet this outcome is very far from being
certain or to be taken for granted, far from being a spontaneous
correlation. Moreover, this theory of individual acting assigns

to the dimension of private interest the function of directing public human relationships. More radically still, it precludes every other way of thinking about social relations, dogmatically dismissing them as illusory or antiliberal. The social actor is left with one way, and only one way, of thinking and acting: the one that has its Archimedean pivot in personal choice and, unless the actors are not shaped by a Protestant ethic, in the principle of ownership.

The second problem is of a sociological kind and pertains to the individualistic nature of society, to the paradoxical fact whereby individualist societies—according to this ideological mode of conceiving individualism—are also those in which there develop communities that are strong, and often exclusive and with a tendency to discriminate against anyone who is not deemed to be similar. Notwithstanding the anticommunitarian assumption, the radical liberalism associated with antipolitical individualism may engender a society that is not only "corporate" but also communitarian in the most anti-individualistic sense of the term, or, to use a telling expression from Sheldon Wolin, as if derived from an inverted totalitarianism.[21] *Possessive-atomistic individualism* and *identitarian individualism* are the two extreme gemmations of a theory that imagines society to be a mechanics of "natural" and spontaneous interactions between actors governed by one and the same instrumental rationality. They are the extreme but not improbable consequences of an antipolitical society, of an idea of the liberty of the moderns as a liberty from politics.

VI

Economic Individualism

The rich and the powerful should not be able to make amends for assaults against the weak and the poor by naming a price; otherwise, wealth, which is the reward of industry under the tutelage of the laws, becomes fodder for tyranny. There is no liberty whenever the laws permit a man in some cases to cease to be a person *and to become a* thing: *then you will see the efforts of the powerful dedicated entirely to eliciting from the mass of civil relations those in which the law is to his advantage. This discovery is the magic secret that transforms citizens into beasts of burden and that, in the hands of the strong, is the chain that fetters the actions of the incautious and the weak. This is why in some governments that have every appearance of liberty, tyranny lies hidden or insinuates itself unseen into some corner neglected by the legislator, where imperceptibly it gathers strength and grows. Generally, men set up the most solid embankments against open tyranny, but they do*

not see the tiny insect that gnaws away at them and opens a path
for the river's flood, a path that is all the more certain to develop
the more hidden it is.

—Cesare Beccaria, 1764

A ntipolitical individualism nurtures a realistic conception of justice that strips of all meaning the very
idea of a just society, a pragmatic utopia, to echo
John Rawls's telling phrase, based upon arguments
from principle that are also constitutional (equal liberties)
and guided by the idea of respect. This form of individualism
destroys the function of democratic politics. While it might
find the first paragraph of article 3 of the Italian Constitution
to be workable—"All citizens have equal social dignity and
are equal before the law, without distinction of sex, race,
language, religion, opinion, and personal and social circumstances"—it would not countenance the wording of the second
paragraph: "It is the task of the Republic to remove obstacles
of an economic and social order that, limiting in practice
the liberty and equality of citizens, obstruct the full development of the human person and the effective participation of
all workers in the social, economic and political organization
of the Country." Reverting to the argument of the liberty of
the moderns as liberty from politics, about which I spoke in
my second chapter, in article 3 two conceptions of political
liberty are encapsulated—in one case it is viewed as a means
to obtain "unmitigated liberty," a liberty that is negative or
that is in the guise of noninterference; in the other, political
liberty has a foundational function as regards associative life

and presupposes citizens who give themselves laws and institutions through which each should be able to "unfurl" his own personality and express his own capacities (human flourishing).[1] In essence, article 3, second paragraph, is a declaration of responsibility on the part of the political community toward its citizens; a declaration of citizenship. It is a recognition of the fact that there exists a political identity—a "we" as a democratic nation—that is committed to acting so as to defend its members as equal beings, in accordance with the promise of liberty sanctioned in the first paragraph of the same article.[2]

But, despite the noble intentions of those who drafted the Italian Constitution, the relationship between these two ideas of liberty is problematic because it implies two different conceptions of the individual and two different visions of what are or ought to be the objectives of democratic society. I propose to shed light upon this awkward relationship by viewing it from a perspective that may well appear extreme, and is at any rate unfamiliar, namely, that of tyranny. Precisely on account of its paradoxical nature, however, this approach may serve to open up interesting prospects for analysis regarding the risks to democratic liberty incubated within modern society. My purpose in the present chapter is to argue that the ideology of economic individualism may well nurture the tyranny of the moderns. Employing the paradigmatic distinction between liberty of the ancients and liberty of the moderns, I propose to reverse the terms of the argument and to focus upon the difference between their respective negations. This is an extreme yet entirely legitimate approach: indeed, if it is true that the liberty of the moderns is essentially private, it is presumably the private sphere that we should consider if we wish to seek out the source of its tyrannical contrary.

A number of preliminary questions may help to clarify the radical nature and the analytical legitimacy of the problem: is it still meaningful to speak of tyranny in the modern democracies? Is it perhaps not the case that written constitutions and the representative system have successfully neutralized the possibilities, if not the temptations, of despotism? The antinomy between ancients and moderns is highly instructive in this regard.

The myth of tyrannicide was foundational for the direct democracy of the ancients, a sign of its intrinsic limits and hence of the need for a symbolic strategy that fixed in the memory of the city the idea of the enemy within and of the antityrannical foundations of the government of the *demos*. This myth demonstrates that direct democracy has never succeeded in incorporating enemies; elsewhere has always remained a possibility projected and at times realized. Thus, in 337–336 B.C., the assembly at Athens passed the *nomos* of Eukrates, as it was known, whereby the city enjoined the Areopagites (the most authoritative magistrates) in the event of subversion of the political order to return to their houses and revert to being private citizens, or not to remain in the service of the tyrants, to not pass or implement antidemocratic laws; were they to do otherwise, at the restoration of democracy they would be tried and condemned to death for treason.[3] Democracy was declaring its own authority beyond its imperium; it was declaring that outside it there was no legitimate order and that its legitimacy was therefore meta-institutional. This proves that in direct democracy the object of contention between democrats and their enemies remained unresolved and unaltered: this object was the right of free adult males to sit in the assembly and in the council, to vote on the laws, and to judge. The law that protected and honored tyrannicide, the one that regulated ostracism or, finally, the one that asserted the authority of democracy beyond itself, served to demonstrate that enemies were never integrated into the democratic political game. The problem was fundamentally numerical, as Aristotle admitted in the *Politics*, where for this reason he sought to find a mediation between oligarchy and democracy, correcting arithmetical equality by means of a system of plural voting that might neutralize the quantitative imbalance between the many (the poor) and the few (the powerful).

The problem, then, was the place of the few, as Machiavelli had clearly grasped when in the *Discorsi* he reminded the enemies of government by the multitude that it was not the many who had the desire to wield power and play an active part in politics, but the few. The many are content simply to know that they are secure in their personal liberty, in their possessions, in their enjoyment of domestic tranquillity and of their work. Not to be dominated is sufficient for the many, but the same is not true of the few or the "great." These latter, for their part, have to be able to satisfy their passion for power; and the good *ordini*, Machiavelli warned, are those that are capable of containing the *hybris dominandi* of the few through a system of supervision and participation that involves the many; or, to echo James Madison, through checks and balances and representation, disrupting the monopoly of power through a process of pluralism set in motion by the politics of rights. If, as Robert Dahl confirmed with great analytical clarity in the 1950s, the few and not the many are the problem,[4] it would then seem legitimate to suppose that the modern democracies have triumphed over their natural political enemies. Their winning strategy has been, rather than a written constitution, representation, because, as the American federalists discerned, it satisfies the interest of the many in monitoring those who exercise power and that of the few in not finding themselves invariably in the minority and in satisfying their passion for power and their resistance to equality. The winning strategy, I would further note, has been that of applying to politics and to institutions the culture of limits and of preemptive limitation—in other words, through norms that had *depressive* effects upon the passion for power of the few and *tonic* effects upon the tendency of the many to withdraw from public affairs in order to enjoy private liberty. This has neutralized the possibility of political tyranny. It has not, however, eliminated the sources of tyranny, or of what Madison calls the unlimited passion for the expansion of influence over the whole of society: *a passion that arises in the private sphere*, and in a particular fashion in the economic domain and in the area of religion. Money and God were the two obstacles that, if left unsupervised, had the power to overturn the constitutional liberty of the moderns. It was therefore crucial that this passion not cross the boundaries of the social and that it not seize hold of the levers of political power. Marking out the boundaries between the private or social sphere and the public sphere has been the aim of the culture of limits implemented by representative and constitutional democracy.

Numerous doubts as to the retentive qualities of these boundaries arise when one considers the site of power in modern democracies, in other words, not the site in which laws are made (as is the case with the power of the sovereign will) but the one through which there is formed the opinion that exercises an indirect influence over those who are elected to make the laws and over those who elect. If in antiquity the risk of tyranny came from the side of the sovereign will (depriving citizens of the right to sit in the assembly), in modern society the risk seems to come from the side of opinion and the formation of political judgment, or from within civil society itself, the workshop within which both opportunities and inequalities are forged, and where the political languages by means of which interests and passions open up a path toward the state are fashioned. Bobbio warned that the power of economic interests combined with the decline in the political or civic education of citizens might give rise to a mixture lethal to representative democracy: the formation of an oligarchical power that could moreover win legitimization through a public opinion rendered docile, uncritical, and passive or else kept in ignorance and rendered incompetent to judge.[5] In any case, representative democracy has shifted outside the state the power of the few to interfere in decisions and to monopolize, if they are able, the political game. Now, if for ancient democracy it was valid to speak of tyranny as a system of arbitrary power that was directly and violently imposed upon the legitimate one (which is how Plato and Aristotle saw it), for modern democracy it seems anachronistic to employ this paradigm precisely for the reasons adduced above regarding the success of the constitutional and representative response to the risk of subversion. It may, however, be more useful to revert to thinking about individualism, since it is precisely from the nonpolitical or private, moral, and social sphere that today the antidemocratic risk may come. Civil society, the site of interests and of the liberty of the moderns, is where we should look for the factors with the potential to subvert government. Let us once again address the question of the character of classical economics, that is, the kind that is descended from the nineteenth-century doctrine of laissez-faire (the "radical free-trade school"). To Max Weber two values were in play here. Without a doubt, Weber said, classical economics was inspired by the wholly justified need to produce a "nonstatist" (in other words, apolitical) "pure theory," which was value free and "individualistic" in method. Problems, however, arose when some of its adepts began to construe it as an "ought to be," that is, as a prescriptive doctrine according to which economic action should become as far as possible a faithful "copy" of " 'natural' reality," or in other words a thing not "distorted by human stupidity," by the irrationality represented by individual desires, by the opinions of the Forum and even by moral demands themselves.[6] In short, the ideology of the free market, not economic science, would be the problem contained in what we today call free-trade doctrine. It is in this perspective that economic individualism needs to be revisited in order to grasp its critical potential in relation to democratic rules and principles.

Now, when commenting upon the Weberian separation between "pure" economic science and dogmatic free-trade doctrine, Steven Lukes has proposed that we challenge the very idea of economics being a "pure science," since, despite its traditional claim to be value free, this discipline is "inherently" normative inasmuch as it presupposes the core institutions of capitalism—private property, the market, free competition—as institutions that "meet the requirement of efficiency and equity" and that therefore are to all intents and purposes a "political *desideratum*," an ought-to-be to be pursued (with the employment of political power, if necessary) rather than simply a neutral and objective description of how things are.[7]

As a *desideratum*, economic individualism does not only call for minimal interference on the part of politics but, even prior to that, dictates to politics the rules governing what a good social order ought to be, an order that assigns to economic self-interest a priority not only as to strategy but also as to value over and against all the other dimensions of life and over all other interests; finally, over the political dimension itself, or over democracy. Here we have to do with a reductionism that may not fairly be imputed to the founder of political economy, Adam Smith, who, though he criticized restrictions upon the free market on the part of the state, was opposed to state intervention for pragmatic, and not for dogmatic reasons (he was not so opposed when it was a question of safeguarding the existence of certain fundamental, and noneconomic, goods, such as, for example, aesthetic ones). The problematic outcome of economistic reductionism is to define as assaults upon liberty all decisions that are the fruit of the human will in collective decision-making contexts: such as rules and social legislation.

I propose now to examine the idea according to which the discipline of the market not only presides over a just distribution of costs and benefits but also is able to regulate itself without interventions from the outside; that is, to restrict the unlimited tendency toward expansion that the American federalists had with great perspicacity foreseen. According to this idea, in other words, the market would by itself be capable of maintaining itself in perpetual motion, demonstrating to economic actors that it is in any case more convenient if there are many alternatives rather than just the one, even if the elimination of competitors is the primary aim and the one desired by all. If the mainspring of the market economy is the aspiration to indefinite growth in a war in which no prisoners are taken, its capacity to persist resides in the fact that no one can win that war. The paradox of "economic progress" in the guise of material growth or an indefinite accumulation of profits, the liberal Mill explained, is that it issues from the awareness that material wealth is not without limits and that growth is not endless. The limitless tendency toward growth can therefore be defined as a ceaseless postponing of its own negation, which does not so much consist in crisis (which is, after all, a form of movement and in any case an anticipated event) as rather in the stationary state—stagnation and the interruption of growth are the radical contrary to the perennial movement of which the market economy consists. For the capitalists as for the economists of the "old school," Mill wrote, the stationary state serves as a warning of which economic actors stand in need if they are to sustain their energies and preempt stasis, while nevertheless being fully aware that there is no escaping that fate, there is merely procrastination. In the *Communist Party Manifesto* of Marx and Engels, as in Mill's *Principles of Political Economy*, the reader is faced with the inevitability of movement, and with the inexorable tendency toward a growth in profits, innovation, and indefinite accumulation, as the forces that sustain and at the same consume capitalist society. This is the philosophy that bolsters self-regulation; a choice that is, however, anything but value free because it reflects an out-and-out law of survival, and one that only in this sense may be said to be natural; the logic of survival is the end that serves to justify the means, precisely as happens, as we shall shortly see, in the realistic conception of politics.[8]

The culture and language of this individualism are at once total and totalizing; its relationship with democratic society is the enduring and still unresolved problem of the modern constitutional state. The founding fathers of liberalism themselves sensed that democracy (representative government) and economic liberalism might well be on a collision course. This is true not only of an author "contaminated" by social democracy such as Hans Kelsen, to whom we owe a categorical distinction between political and economic liberalism (it not necessarily being possible to equate the latter with democracy), but also of Constant, an author profoundly convinced that modern society allows greater personal liberty, thanks also to the economics of exchange.[9] Constant, in the discourse on the liberty of the ancients and of the moderns I mentioned in chapter 2, placed the emphasis upon money as the cause of the radical diversity between these two worlds. Money—and Constant proved remarkably perceptive here—has a double value with regard to society: on the one hand, by liberating property from every personal determination and hence from the identification with landed property, it liberates individuals from personal power relations and politics from despotic domesticity; on the other hand, it uproots property from every form of belonging and divests it of every ethical and political loyalty. The ownership principle of modern society is based upon the depersonalization of the moral and economic relationships between individuals, and likewise between the individuals themselves and nature; it creates an abstract dimension of norms that serves as a means of communication between autonomous social actors and one that is outside, or beyond, the direct intervention of the coercive power of the state; or, as we saw in the previous chapter, one that follows a process of self-regulation.

Constant produced a very effective synthesis of these two contradictory tendencies. He observed that "money," though it could well become one of the "most dangerous weapons of despotism . . . is at the same time its most powerful restraint."[10] Indeed, in money there materialized a peculiarly modern power, that of opinion or trust. Exchanges, banking credit, and commerce are in fact conditioned by the social and political order, in the sense that they function best where the political institutions are governed by fixed rules and laws in which trust in stability, regularity, and transparency is rooted. This interdependence between money and opinion, between voluntary exchanges and a civil society that is mobile and regulated by

law, serves as an important antidiote to liberticide governments
and the arbitrariness of the sovereign will. However, Constant
further observed, property and money are not the same thing;
and the priority of money over landed or immobile property
inevitably leads to the alienation of individual ownership, with
regard not only to productive labor but also to political belonging to country or nation.

When men engaged in commerce and finance have
achieved peace and quiet and can expand undisturbed, as occurs
in free societies and under constitutional governments, they
tend to exert a somewhat radical influence upon human relationships, private and public, and this influence may jeopardize
the very same free institutions that money needs in order to
establish equivalence between incomparable goods and hence
to be an effective means of exchange. A similar argument led
Kant to write that the indebtedness of countries may be a wor-
rying factor serving to limit the independence of decision
making in governments and hence the political liberty of citizens, with grave consequences for international stability and
peace: and it would enable Marx to explain the dictum *l'argent
n'a pas de maître*—or, as we would say, "money has no color"—
as an example of the embeddedness in popular culture of the
idea that money has a power above that of men; it has more
power than the law itself of states, a power that so transcends
the will that it assumes the character of divinity.[11]

Here then we find, according to Constant, and in yet
another sense, money and opinion to be linked: in the sense
that money holds political opinion in check because it establishes its own priorities without being concerned for the
best interests of the country. Thus politics prostrates itself before, and seeks to respond to, the demands of finance. "Credit
did not have the same influence among the ancients; their

governments were stronger than individuals, while in our time individuals are stronger than the political powers. Wealth is a power which is more readily available in all circumstances, readily applicable to all interests, and consequently more real and better obeyed. Power threatens; wealth rewards . . .," and if it should fail to triumph over political opinion it will then resort to the weapon of flight. Without armies and blood, money gets itself "served" like the most ruthless of tyrants.[12] There was in fact a none too veiled criticism in Constant's words, since his analysis did not say that the liberty of the moderns is superior or that the political life of the ancient republics is of less value: in a more subtle fashion he intimates that what "suited" the moderns was different from what "suited" the ancients.[13]

For the liberals of the first half of the nineteenth century, raised upon classical rhetoric and philosophy, politics was still public service and a public good rather than a career; the opposite stance, where it was encountered, was a shortcoming to be corrected (and a thing generally equated with Machiavellianism) rather than a necessity to which one should submit. Notwithstanding his fundamental defense of individual liberty, Constant reaffirmed the centrality of the attachment of citizens to the customs of the "forefathers" as a condition of the liberty of the moderns. For this reason, no differently from the ancients, and certainly no differently from Aristotle or Cicero, he assigned great value to property in land and mistrusted financial profit, although he was a sincere and altogether staunch defender of property rights and of the free market.

Property in land, for Constant as for his contemporary Hegel, bound the individual to his own homeland with bonds of self-interest and of memories, so that it was correct to say that property and fatherland were mutually reinforcing—just as the liberty of the individual and that of the citizen were. Yet

financial capital or property deriving from commerce prospered
to such a degree that an individual was naturally indifferent to
the fate of, and to circumstances prevailing in, his own country.
Commerce knows no borders, and indeed it prompts the individual to uproot himself from any communitarian ties, transferring, for example, his place of residence to wherever is most
convenient, or even starving his own people, if he should happen to profit by that. The nature of the soil, and the variations
in climate, history, and collective memories, in short, the natural and human environment, have no meaning for the man of
business; his compass is gain and accumulation, and there is
no limit to them save vanity, a wholly private passion and, to
revert to the theme of the attributes of the tyrannical individual, one that is unlimited in nature. This explains, among
other things, the preference shown by the moderns for living
"concentrated in the capital": since, along with the need for
money, there they feel a growing need to curry favor with the
politicians and then to win recognition from their fellows. For
liberals such as Constant, Mill, and Tocqueville, these were the
passions that drove the individualist to refine economic calculation, and to create at the last an exquisitely modern type of
tyrant. Except for the fact that their opinion may be recognized
in the words of a classical author: "There is indeed no limit to
the amount of riches to be got from this mode of acquiring
goods. . . . So, while it seems that there must be a limit to every
form of wealth, in practice we find that the opposite occurs: all
those engaged in acquiring goods go on increasing their coin
without limit."[14]

There is no doubt that for these influential liberals
individualism was the highest cost that the liberty of the moderns had to pay. We read in Constant's *The Spirit of Conquest
and Usurpation* that when the tie with territory comes to be

sundered and residence is simply an expedient and a function of one's own interests, both being dissociated from participation in civil and political life, individuals are then seized by ambition and "lost in an unnatural isolation, strangers in the place of their birth, without contact with the past, living only in a hasty present, cast like atoms upon an immense, flat plain, [they] detach themselves from a fatherland that they can nowhere see."[15] In this fashion there was consolidated a false notion of liberty, which was not self-mastery but the love of ownership, of consumption and of appearance, the modern and more refined forms, as Rousseau had noted, of a new dependence, of a wholly modern despotism that was born of subjugation to the opinion of others, of living in obedience to a principle external to their reason, just like the slaves of antiquity in relation to their lord, to the *despotes*. Industrial property "does not have as a necessary component that slow, safe progress which creates the habit, and soon the need for uniformity. It does not make a man independent of other men. On the contrary, it places him in their dependence."[16]

The author of the distinction between the liberty of the ancients and the liberty of the moderns, despite the fact that he had very firmly declared the latter to be an advance on the former, when he addressed the causes of the decline of citizens' interest in the public good and, consequently, of the corruption of the political class, factors among other things of the recurrent revolutions in Europe, therefore nursed serious doubts as to the value of a life absorbed in the quest for personal satisfaction and for accumulation. Modern society, when considered from the point of view of uniformity of value (ownership), resembled the bourgeois family depicted by Honoré de Balzac, with one class (men/capitalists) dedicated to success and in exclusive domination of the public sphere, and the other (women/workers) reduced to the condition of pariah, deprived of the opportunity to satisfy those same "bourgeois" passions of ambition and of a career that competition promoted and celebrated.[17]

We have thus arrived at the end point anticipated at the beginning of the chapter. For these liberal authors antipolitical individualism was synonymous at one and the same time with tyranny and with alienation, with an insatiable vanity but also with an apolitical "calm and considered feeling," to use Tocqueville's telling phrase, with indifference toward the fate of society, a monstrous phenomenon that had, he thought, unforeseeable implications. Above all, this individualism forged a tyrannical "ego," a mixture of greedy and acquisitive license and, at the same time, of dependence upon the logic of accumulation, and, finally, upon others, upon the needs and upon the opinions of the Forum. These liberal authors took their cue from two classical texts in particular: the *Republic* of Plato and the *Politics* of Aristotle, works containing canonical passages for anyone seeking the key to the psychology and morality of the individual-tyrant and of despotism. I shall end this chapter with a brief account of the former, and then revert to the latter in the next chapter.

The tyrant individual is the predominant theme in the *Republic*, the obsession to which the quest of Plato's Socrates for the best form of government and education is anchored. The question around which the dialogue turns has to do with the nature of justice. The dialogue begins with the presentation of some conceptions of justice (voiced by Polemarchus and Cephalus), only for its calm and measured flow to be interrupted by the bursting onto the scene of Thrasymachus, the anti-Socrates. For Socrates, Thrasymachus is a veritable obsession, and the reply to him takes up ten whole books of the

Platonic dialogue. Thrasymachus is the epitome of the tyrant individual, but also of the vision that the laissez-faire individualist has cultivated: to the effect that the rules of justice are value free and natural; that every prescriptive discourse on justice construed as a matter of reasonable relationships for the general good is nothing but ideology or a pipedream.

Thrasymachus epitomizes the tyrant in his verbal style, in his relationship with his interlocutors, and, finally, in his conception of life and of politics. The Platonic conception of justice and of the good constitution rests upon the parallel between the individual soul and the city. The performance of Thrasymachus is designed to unmask the logic underpinning Plato's analogical strategy: every individual is like a citadel in which the tyrant and the just man confront one another, and every individual is the outcome of an action of the government upon his own emotions and passions, an action of moderation if not of repression, an action of limitation that is not easily made concrete or, above all, given shape and consistently maintained. Every individual is therefore at risk of becoming a tyrant, and for this reason every constitution is subject to the risk of degeneration. But the well-ordered city is one that facilitates the education of the reasonable part of the individual and contains or keeps in check the tyrannical part: the unrestrained passion for the accumulation of goods and powers, of honors and of admiration. It is against this theory that Thrasymachus vents his fury. He had remained silent for the whole of the first part of the dialogue, displaying, however, signs of impatience until "he could keep quiet no longer; But gathering himself up like a wild beast he sprang at us as if he would tear us to pieces."[18] Thrasymachus then explodes. He does not enter into a dialogue but declaims, shouts; he imposes his truth with an almost bestial force. If he cannot tolerate dialogue, it is because he has nothing to dialogue about; he must not alter his ideas inasmuch as he already knows what the truth is, and it would be meaningless for him to seek to convince his interlocutors, in that the truth he has to tell prevails in every single case, owing to the naturalness of things (and it is this logic of naturalness that accounts for a stance that is bestial and inimical to civilized life, a life created through artificial and unnatural rules, in short, through *nomos* and not *physis*). He then inveighs against Socrates, saying that he it is who is the real manipulator, since he leads his interlocutor a merry dance, inducing him to admit whatsoever he wishes. In this confrontation with the master of irony, Thrasymachus seeks redemption: he, who is as candid and clear as nature is, does not manipulate but tells; he does not play with rigged questions but gives answers that are difficult to object to. He transforms Socratic irony from something employing a rhetorical figure to say jokingly the opposite—so as to induce one's interlocutor to delve into the meaning of words and concepts—into a veritable art of dissimulation, of deception. But Thrasymachus does not deceive: his version of justice has no need of any play upon words and lengthy disquisitions because it is self-evident, and those who reject it confess to being prey to moralistic prejudices. The manipulator is the person who, like Socrates, says that justice is the good of the community masking the truth. But justice is what the person with the most power says that it is: it is the law of the strongest.

Thrasymachus's justice resides not in the society in which the law holds sway over men but in the one in which men impose their law with whatever instruments are most appropriate, whether violence or speech. The fact is that, according to the logic of Thrasymachus, it is not possible to make any distinction between these two forms of society, since always and in any case it is the power of the strongest that commands (even when he hides his intentions behind beguiling utopias). The social class with the most economic power, Marx would explain many centuries later, casts government in its own image and likeness, and turns its own justice into a universal norm, decreeing what justice is. The political game is a rhetorical game: it consists of successfully convincing the masses, so that each person, having been a potential adversary and critic, becomes a friend and advocate.

Having blurted out his truth, Thrasymachus disappears from the dialogue once and for all. But his absence serves as a pole star, because it is to Thrasymachus that Socrates wishes to, and must, reply, and it is against Thrasymachus that he defines justice and the good political order; indeed, to preempt the emergence of a Thrasymachus, of a man in the likeness of a "beast," an individual who does not countenance dissent because he asserts the truth as a natural law, who uses mockery to cast aspersions on those who think, who jeers at every rule and every principle because he sees in the law and in the constitution an insupportable limitation upon his will and power; who indeed declares that all laws and norms are an expression of the power of the strongest, of whoever can impel obedience, of whoever enjoys the majority of plaudits and is therefore delegated to act. It is not the law that commands obedience, nor is it dialogue that has the power to convince anyone to obey a just law; the capacity to command obedience lies with those who have the power to impose it, a physical power in some cases, and a power inhering in symbols and in speech in others, and an economic power in yet others.

Thrasymachus's discourse is a veritable hymn to realism and to an instrumental relativism of values. Whoever crams his mouth full of values such as justice and respect for others is either a useless and ineffectual preacher or a cunning manipulator who uses these values as an art of enchantment to dominate by imposing belief, and to subjugate with the consent of those subordinated to him. For the realist Thrasymachus, Socrates's irony is all this and more. Thrasymachus is perhaps the first theorist of ideology as a calculated art of winning consent for a predictable end: the conquest of, and the preservation of power, irrespective of whether it is on the part of an individual or of a group. Politics, force, and justice are all one and the same.

The logic of realism survives the centuries unscathed, and enjoys a moment of great brilliance in the shape of Hobbes, and then through the ideology of "true" economic individualism. In all such cases, as in that of Thrasymachus, every distinction between forms of government is in principle devoid of meaning since, whatever the regime, the law must be obeyed and whoever holds power has the strength to impose obedience; because, finally, the transformation of the law from arbitrary act to norm is simply the outcome of an ideological exercise underlying which there is the self-interest of the strongest; in the modern case, economic liberty is the direction that holds in its hands the strings of society and that turns governments from despotic to liberal, because it is only in nondespotic governments, as Montesquieu has explained, that commerce flourishes, availing itself of social relations based upon the regularity and predictability of norms rather than upon the unpredictable will of a tyrant. In this case too liberty serves the interests of the strongest:

> Every government lays down laws [*nomoi*] for its own advantage—a democracy democratic, a tyranny tyrannical laws, and so on. In laying down these laws they have made it plain that what is to

their advantage is just. They punish anyone who
goes against this as a law-breaker and an unjust
man. This, then, is what I say justice is, the same in
all cities. It is what is advantageous to the established government. But the established government is master, and so sound reasoning gives the
conclusion that the same thing is always just—
namely, what is advantageous to the stronger.[19]

For Thrasymachus, then, all regimes are equivalent, and
in a democracy the majority has the same absolute power that
the individual tyrant has in a tyranny. Advancing arguments
for good government is an activity devoid of meaning: insofar
as it is able to impose its own command, every government
is good. Duration ratifies its goodness, while domestic tranquillity is an index of its acceptance and consequently of the well-
being of the society. That is how it is in a society founded upon
consent and public opinion, such as modern society, where
the apathy of the citizens is an index of their acceptance of
the government. This then is, from Thrasymachus onward, the
heart of moral positivism, of the idea that judgments of justice
are always and in any case judgments of existence, not of value,
and that they are dictates internal to the natural mechanism of
interests. This, according to Plato's Socrates, is the logic underlying the philosophy of the tyrant individual: the identification
of the norm with *his* law. Justice is simply the logic of the victor.

VII

Apathy and Solitude

*[Tyrannies adopt] every means for making every subject as much
of a stranger as is possible to every other. (Mutual acquaintance
always tends to create mutual confidence.) . . . [And they] require
every resident in the city to be constantly appearing in public. . . .
(This is meant to give the ruler a peep-hole into the actions of his
subjects, and to inure them to humility by a habit of daily slavery.)*

—Aristotle, Politics, 1313b

I f, to take up Tocqueville's thread once again, egoism is a
moral shortcoming as old as the world itself, a vice from
which the passion for ownership, and hence economic
progress, derives sustenance according to the logic of the
heterogeneity of ends, individualism for its part is a political
phenomenon that may result in indifference toward society and

public affairs. From the tyrant individual one thus passes to the invisible and apathetic individual, a totally private individual not because he would wish to subjugate the public to his interests but rather because he avoids taking part in public life in order to take refuge outside politics and to remain on the margins of the *polis*. The modern tyrant arises in the private sphere of economics and reflects the two sides of the private individual: an overweening self-esteem above and against all others (the individual as *prius* with respect to society) and a conception of the public as simply a means to acquire something of purportedly greater importance, namely, the accumulation and safeguarding of personal goods, above all those that are economic. Although differing in their manifestations and implications, these are the two possible forms assumed by the inclination to reject politics that modern democracy may engender. The first to describe the privatization of life as the sign of a despotic form of rule over society was Aristotle, in the second book of the *Politics*, in the context of a critique of the Platonic ideal of the republic as a harmonious unity of individuals who were identical and devoid of individual specificity, because private in their economic interests and in their personal ties and in their sympathies. In order to render the city just and to pacify it, Plato had expelled from politics anyone who concerned himself with social affairs, and from social affairs anyone who concerned himself with politics; the former he had deprived of any voice in government, the latter he had denied property and family, or, in other words, the causes behind partiality of judgment and hence injustice. The paradox laid bare by Aristotle—which anticipates the earliest critiques of the totalitarian temptation implicit in the privatization of politics—was that an exclusively public life ended up destroying the public by rendering it mimetic of the private: the entirely equal guardians of Plato's *Republic* ended up not being distinguishable one from the other because there was nothing to differentiate them, not even their emotions, given that they had been educated in an identical fashion from an early age so as to have the selfsame feelings; they ended up finally being entirely uninterested in one another precisely because lacking in any relationship of interest or feeling through which they might claim some specificity. Their being identical made them indifferent both to others and to the good of the city. Paradoxically, the Platonic utopia turned the entire city into a family even as it sought to wrest citizens from their families.

The contradiction laid bare by Aristotle implied that a city incapable of sustaining individual liberty in the moral and social sphere is incapable of cultivating political liberty. In a city reduced to a unit of the familial type, individuals cease to have any place, whether as private individuals or as citizens. The precondition of politics lies in the possibility of citizens having a private life distinct from and distinguishable from public life, in their capacity to practice the art of making a distinction.

It is interesting to observe how, in his critique of Plato's totalizing republic, which loses the character of the state, because it reduces "harmony to unison, or . . . a theme to a single beat,"[1] Aristotle's case hinges upon private, not political virtues when challenging the republic of the guardians; he asserts moral liberty even before politics. Yet his strategy is indubitably political, because the impoverishment of individuality entailed by the stifling of the pluralism of styles of life may engender the atrophy of public life and of liberty itself.

The rule of liberty, Aristotle suggested, is the coexistence of public and private, not their mutual exclusion, that is to say, the fact that the private and the public individual, the person and the citizen, are able to coexist within one and the same person. In order to eliminate the causes of crises, such as corruption and apathy, the public power cannot turn subjects into soulless functionaries: nor, conversely, can it make the private life of citizens public. It is no accident that Jeremy Bentham should have taken his cue from Platonic logic when devising what may be defined as the first systematic vision of the modern prison system construed in terms of depersonalization through the abolition of the private—the abolition of secrecy, with the light of day being brought to bear upon every aspect of the intimate and personal life of the inmates: in his Panopticon the detainees lived under identical conditions and were treated all the same; they were permanently exposed to the vigilant eye of an unseen supervisor; overall they constituted a portrait *ante litteram* of the democratic despotism feared by Tocqueville, one in which everyone's life was inspected and probed in order to enable the central power to implement efficient policies. Tocqueville had also apprehended at birth the paradoxical implications of power's capacity to probe arising out of the freedom of the press, a necessity for free governments but a thing not devoid of problems precisely because of its nature, that is to say, its being a liberty that could not allow checks on the part of the political authorities without inevitably being destroyed. He had sensed that the loss of the distinction between public and private could be the outcome not of liberticide laws such as those used by the absolute monarchs of the past to humiliate dissidents through torture and spells of imprisonment decided upon irrespective of any juridical guarantees, but rather of laws devised precisely to protect freedom of expression and of speech, a freedom to speak, write, and put things into the public domain. The ultimate and probably unpremeditated outcome of this freedom of judgment and

speech could be the creation in modern society of a new republic of guardians along the lines described by Plato. The making
public or bringing into the public domain of the most intimate
and personal experiences of life, such as affects or moral dilem-
mas, amounts to eroding the private sphere, thereby turning
the organ of publicity—speech, judgment—into the instrument
of the "free" and civic version of the prison system devised by
Bentham.

Let us, then, try to clarify the difference between democratic individualism and this depersonalized individualism,
which, Tocqueville anticipated, persons would shun, taking
refuge in communitarian relationships, outside politics and
away from the public.

From the eighteenth century onward, the defenders of
identitary communities have accused democracy of promoting
an atomistic society; in reply, the theorists of democracy maintain that the value of this society lies in rendering possible the
condition of "solitude" without, however, precluding association
with others for the most disparate reasons, from the promotion
of economic interests or the cultivation of aesthetic pleasures
to the sharing of a religious faith. Thanks to the Constitution
and to the Charter of Rights, this political order enables each
to put a salutary distance, so to speak, between herself as individual and herself as a part of society—to protect her own ideas,
choices, and styles of life from encroachment not only by the
law (political majorities are supposed to halt on the threshold
of rights) but also by the opinion of the "public," a modern
power that operates indirectly, prompting without imposing,
standardizing without compelling; in other words, to protect
the intimate and private dimension of individual life from the
illiberal passions that the entirely comprehensible pursuit of
meaningful identities can provoke, such as communitarian

zeal, hatred of what is different, the "foolish adoration" of one's own sect above and against all others, the reassuring sensation of being able to blend in with one's own group, to identify with it to such a degree that one ends up wholly losing any sense of oneself as a distinct individual.[2] George Herbert Mead wrote that there are two forms of social group that determine the whole and the individuality of the members: the one that pertains to the kingdom of the invertebrates (the termites and the hymenoptera are "societies whose interests determine for the individuals their stimuli and habitats") and the one that pertains to the kingdom of the vertebrates, for whom there does not exist any kind of "inherited physiological differentiation to mediate the complexities of social conduct," and who can cooperate effectively because they internalize actions and the effect they have on others. In these latter, the "so-called herding instinct" is hard put to go beyond a tendency to standardize the actions of individuals. The distance between individual world and environment is characteristic of human societies.[3] Let us add that it is also a peculiar feature of human societies as such that, as in the case of democratic society, they are based upon a majority/minority relationship.

Individualism—in the guise of solitude with respect to society—is in this case the registering not of an absence (of the other) but of a presence (of oneself). As I shall show in the next chapter, Emerson, inviting his readers to mistrust their desire for community, very perceptively observed how it was that each individual dreams up ingenious strategies for protecting himself from the gaze of others, in order to preserve intimacy with himself: solitude, courtesy, good manners, the codes of Galateo, irony, and sarcasm are just some of the expedients to which each of us resorts from time to time to render our "skin" thicker and to keep at bay not so much the contamination exercised by others' ideas as the inspection, the surveillance, and the censorship. The term "solitude" used to refer to the social condition of the modern individual may have at least two meanings, both political, but with different if not opposite implications. In one case, solitude may be interpreted as a protective shield defending one's own autonomy of judgment and as a denunciation of the potentially oppressive character of political power and of those who court and wield it. In the other case, solitude expresses rather a condition of isolation from others, or of atomism. The first to describe solitude as a shield were the American transcendentalist philosophers, above all Emerson, Thoreau, and Whitman, who explicitly interpreted it as a necessary tonic sustaining independence of judgment in a society naturally inclined to homogenize and to reward the prevailing or majority opinion, to penalize diversity and promote anyone who subscribes to the general view of things and who goes with the stream. "One protects himself by solitude, and one by courtesy, and one by an acid, worldly manner,—each concealing how he can the thinness of his skin and his incapacity for strict association. . . . But the necessity of solitude is deeper than we have said, and is organic . . . the people are to be taken in very small doses. If solitude is proud, so is society vulgar. In society, high advantages are set down to the individual as disqualifications. . . . It is not the circumstance of seeing more or fewer people, but the readiness of sympathy, that imports."[4] In order to flee humdrum routine and to cease "slumbering" in the deception of "appearances," Thoreau had decided to take to the woods, where he could live as his wisdom dictated. Yet the simplicity and naturalness he sought was in no sense an act of divorce from society, nor was his moral denunciation of the "false order" intended to presage an unpolitical and wholly private utopia. "I wanted to live deep and suck out all the marrow of life, to live so sturdily and Spartan-like as to put to rout all that was not life" and to accept a "sincere" existence whatever guise it might assume, whether "shabby" or "sublime," without enslaving it to transcendental forces or to social conventions.[5]

The thinker who, on the other hand, viewed solitude as an extraordinary power of isolation rather than association was Bentham, who explicitly identified it with the greatest possible lack of liberty in a society founded upon guarantees of individual liberty. Let us begin by examining the latter. In the Panopticon—which, thanks to Michel Foucault, has become the paradigm of the anomic society that negates individuality even as it creates individualism (a reflection of the world under the sway of Newspeak imagined by George Orwell)—the surveillance by an invisible eye is total and effective precisely because unseen and therefore not susceptible to being controlled or limited, and absolute inasmuch as it does not allow anyone to carve out for himself a space of solitude, a cone of shadow in which to find refuge and to recover some slight sense of being individually distinct. In the *Prison Letters*, Antonio Gramsci described a state of maximal isolation, the lack of a private space in which to be alone, or to abstract himself from an environment which, like "a monstrous machine . . . crushes and levels," breaking up lived time into separate units "like little grains of sand in a gigantic clepsydra." The negation of the private dimension—Orwell's house of glass—was the instrument employed by the Fascist prison authorities to obliterate the prisoners' moral and psychological autonomy, and hence their capacity to resist or to rebel; solitude was thereby turned into isolation, and equality into an indifferent assimilation of subjects who, individually, were "nothing."[6]

What relationship is there between this condition and the acquisitive attitude of which I spoke in the previous chapter? It is once again Bentham who provides us with the answer, since it is to him that we owe the doctrinaire perfecting of the Hobbesian idea that the value of the things for which one competes is measured by the appetite of the competitors. This is Benthamite utilitarianism's point of departure for its claim that every form of association is governed exclusively by "its own conception of what is its own interest, in the narrowest and most selfish sense of the word interest: never by any regard for the interest of the people."[7] Commenting upon this type of individualism, Hannah Arendt has identified it with possessive ethics, for her the origin of the totalitarian individual, precisely on account of its being a doctrine that founds society on isolation and the private individual, a corruption of modern liberalism rather than its fulfillment; the product of the mechanics of mass man that has driven "the dichotomy of public and private functions, of family and work, so far apart that he can no longer find in his person any tie between the two."[8] Upon this vision of individualism critiques of democracy as a government of the crowd have been built. But these are critiques that are based more or less knowingly upon an identification, asserted and not proven, of the "people" with the "mass," an assumption that denies or fails to mention what has in fact been the foundation of democracy since it first made its appearance in Athens: a form of government that rests upon two principles, namely, that each participate in the life of the city and that the political subject should be the single individual and not the masses.

Solitude acquires a positive meaning when it is opposed to a state of isolation. It corresponds to a moral condition of autonomy that individuals seek in a constant attempt to overcome the sense of extraneousness that arises from immersing their minds in the opinions of others, and in their endeavor to restore their faith in themselves, to have the courage of their own ideas, and, finally, to be able to enter into communication with others. It serves to confirm, rather than to disavow, the dialogical nature of human beings. Differentiating between it and isolation, Arendt has effectively identified solitude with the actual precondition of thinking: "Solitude is the human condition in which I keep myself company."[9] Its polar opposite is the state of isolation, which, Gramsci would have said, is tantamount to never being able to be with oneself, to being a monad lacking the possibility of entering into dialogue with itself— "ordinarily it is necessary for me to adopt a dialogical point of view, since otherwise I feel no intellectual stimulus."[10]

But in order to grasp the peculiarity of the apathetic and indifferent individual as a putative product of modern society we must revert to Tocqueville's distinction between individualism and egoism, the former being a political category, the latter a moral one. Here Tocqueville is making analytical and sociological use of Constant's distinction between ancients and moderns. He understands that modern democracy has little in common with the ancient kind, not only because its citizens are moved by the passion for ownership and private happiness, but also because they tend to show scant generosity toward the city and are little disposed to participate in public life; indeed, they avoid political careers, which are therefore the professional preserve of the mediocre and the dishonest—the worst, in other words, not the best; they do not aspire to glory but cultivate their own private security, and this renders politics in such societies neither radical nor turbulent, and above all in no way exposed to the risk of anarchy but if anything inclined to passivity and docility. More than a flight from politics or an anarchical reaction against politics, theirs is a degradation of politics.

We saw in the Introduction how the anarchic nature of the Italians, their perennial use of the maxim "I don't give a damn," has long been attributed to their individualism. Yet if they were anarchic, Tocqueville might have objected, it was precisely because theirs was not an individualist society founded upon equality. Modern democracy is mediocre in the politicians who express it, is very moderate in the decisions it takes, and has a propensity to be apathetic, but it is not anarchic; rebellions are not rife, nor is there even an excess of political activism, because in it there dwell "a lot of orderly, temperate, moderate, careful, and self-controlled citizens."[11] These essentially positive qualities are the natural nutrients both of the culture of respect and rights and of apathy and a climate of indifference. In essence, the greatest shortcoming of democracy flows from one of its undeniable merits. This is the paradox of democratic individualism, a paradox from which one cannot escape without placing the whole system in question, whereas one can stimulate what is valuable through an attempt to educate and to foster participation. In short, as we shall see in the final chapter, democracy corrects itself by means of more democracy; it corrects itself by facilitating, not lambasting, dissent, that is to say, by according consistent recognition to the principle that individual judgment is the foundation of democratic sovereignty.

One may readily understand why, according to Tocqueville, "individualism in democracies" was a new idea and why it had to be distinguished from egoism. The difference between egoism and individualism is grasped and interpreted in relation to democratic citizenship and therefore to politics. "Egoism sterilizes the seeds of every virtue; individualism at first only dams the spring of public virtues." The one is a perverse passion, "a passionate and exaggerated love of self" and a "blind instinct" that leads one to refer everything to oneself and to prefer oneself to all the rest. The other has a mainly political meaning because it is "a calm and considered feeling," a disposition of the mind, not a passion; it stems not from an instinct but from a "misguided judgment"; not from a "depraved feeling" but almost from a calculation of convenience, and it grows like a "vice" of the mind so as gradually to become a "vice" of the heart. It may happen that, habituated to thinking that their rights are secure because all effortlessly respect the laws, democratic citizens are impelled by their own liberty itself toward a kind of indifference toward the public to whom they owe that liberty; and this, in the long run, may give rise to a progressive deterioration in that same culture of rights, transformed ever more readily into the mistaken idea that liberty means doing whatever one wants—and here the maxim "I don't give a damn" returns—so that in the end individualism "attacks and destroys" all the virtues, the private ones no less than the public ones, "and finally merges in egoism."[12]

The cycle of individualism closes when individualism sheds every semblance of the political and returns to its starting point: the notion of individual liberty as liberty from politics, which, from Constant onward, had been identified as the proper condition for the happiness of the moderns. Hence, the more citizens withdraw from public life in order to occupy themselves with their personal concerns, since individual rights serve their purpose here, the more the feeling of solidarity with others declines, the more that quality of empathy which, as we have seen, is among the components of democratic individualism, dries up, the more the political order is exposed to the risks of despotism and a curtailment of liberty, not through an excess of politics, but through an atrophying of politics. This is a despotism that assumes precisely democratic society's own characteristics: the despotism not of a person but of a caste (the caste of elected politicians) and above all of a pervasive public opinion that drives the social mechanism and molds tastes and ideas, metabolizing the differences and diluting the specificity of individuals.

Individualism in democratic societies may lead a citizen to deprive herself of politics. It may coincide with the citizen's abandonment of public space that, precisely on account of its being administered, is felt to be like a prison, a domain in which individual actions have no power and state structures have a life of their own, impersonal, distant, and deaf to the reasons and decisions of individual citizens. With equality and popular sovereignty there may then spring up a "dogma" that seems to fool individuals into dissolving every political obligation without thus, they fondly suppose, losing liberty (is it not they perhaps who are the sovereign?) and into dedicating themselves to themselves with an exclusive and jealous devotion. "Democracy loosens social ties, but it tightens natural ones. At the same time as it separates citizens, it brings kindred closer together."[13] The more the capacity to influence the life of society as individuals diminishes (since the principle of one head, one vote can imply the idea of the pointlessness of electoral participation), the more private initiative and the determination to think for themselves grows, to concern themselves with their own lives in the sphere in which they can be certain of wielding some influence, of having some way of verifying the effects of their own decisions and choices. A confirmation of Tocqueville's intuition came from Emerson, an author whose name does not feature in *Democracy in America*, although he was already well known as a thinker and preacher in the Boston area when Tocqueville visited it. Emerson sensed that it was the condition itself of liberty that rendered every communitarian trust obsolete, and

conversely lent luster to this new form of heroism, that of the
solitude of the common man. "The social sentiments are weak.
The sentiment of Patriotism is weak. Veneration is low. . . . There
is an universal resistance to ties and ligaments once supposed
essential to civil society. [The new age] . . . tends to solitude."[14]
Solitude stood here for liberty; it meant a refusal, of precisely
the kind that had been demanded by the religious reformers, to
countenance any "mediation" whatsoever between oneself and
the truth. Regrets for a past of solid and clear social or caste
affiliations, or recriminations against the vulgarization of politics, were for Emerson nothing more than the legacy of forms
of life alien to individualist society: visions of homogeneity and
of collective identification, or of a permanent political activism.

    If, then, individualism is political, it is because it arises
from a considered feeling of individual impotence in a society
founded upon political equality, of one's own paltry weight as
a single citizen when weighed in the balance against that of the
body of citizens. As twentieth-century political scientists have
repeatedly demonstrated, the power of a single unit such as an
individual vote is so trifling, and the sense a citizen has of in-
fluencing political choices so slight, that the decision not to
participate will not be rationally thought to be a loss, nor conversely will the decision to participate be viewed as a gain. The
logic of the free rider, explained by Mancur Olson in 1965, is
the outcome of the individualism seen as a "calm and considered
feeling" of which Tocqueville spoke, and electoral abstention is
the tangible evidence of the political nature of individualism
(the logic of the free rider is naturally applicable to the fiscal
behavior of tax dodgers, and likewise to anyone who more
generally shirks her civic duty, for example by abstaining from
voting: "Since there are those who do participate or pay taxes I
am not compromising anything if I do not go out to vote or if

I do not pay," where it is plain that if all were to behave thus society would collapse and, finally, the same individual would find her interests ill-served).[15]

The "reasonable" liberty of the moderns, Constant had maintained, is "private" liberty, a "pleasure of reflection" rather than a "pleasure of action" alongside others, unless the others are "neighbors," as the members of an association, friends, or colleagues with a shared interest or in the same lobby group are. Through indifference to politics, concerted action with others on account of the logic of sentimental proximity or closeness of interests and opinions may become an active expression of *antipolitics*, a quest for a way of living that is not only within the private sphere but for the private sphere, its interests and its intrinsic values. After due consideration, then, Tocqueville concluded, as we have seen, that the cycle of individualism closed with a return to egoism: a "passionate" preference for oneself or for one's group, which leads one to "refer everything to oneself" and to turn politics to one's own advantage. The role of politics as participation of the sovereign citizens in the life of society, in politics, having been scaled down, it is to politics nonetheless that this individualist returns us, on the basis of the identity and closeness with the world into which one has withdrawn in order to derive comfort from relationships with one's fellows: one's personal interests, "one's family and one's friends."

Tocqueville does not say that among the possible risks of the individualism that assumes the guise of political egoism there could be either the return to patrimonialism (an economic privacy that absorbs the public, turning it into its opportunistic instrument) or the identitarian celebration of local communities (another typology of subjugation of the public to a private end). I intend to spell out this interpretation in the next chapter, and I wish to do so setting out precisely from the words I have quoted from Tocqueville: "Democracy loosens social ties, but it tightens natural ones. At the same time as it separates citizens, it brings kindred closer together." Above all else, it interrupts the weave and weft of memory and time, causing "each man to forget his ancestors" and by the same token his "descendants," both separated from contemporaries, the only sovereigns or actors to which reference is in this circumstance made. The antipolitical solution to individualism viewed as a shortcoming of the democratic citizen is therefore interpretable as the consequence of an erosion of political temporality, which is based in memory, as Burke had suggested in his critique of the rationalistic and antihistorical justification of human rights: the memory of past generations who have helped to build up the liberties and the guarantees upon which the citizens of the present construct their private and public life, bequeathing the fruits of them to their descendants, through a chain of memories that keeps everyone united, in time and in space. Such, according to Burke, was the unity of the nation, and not the social contract imagined by the followers of Rousseau. Breaking the "weft of time," making presentism the condition of individual life: in these phenomena Tocqueville suggests that we locate the genesis of democratic despotism, an extreme form of antipolitics because it is not merely a revulsion against participation but above all a reconfiguration of politics itself as administrative bricolage, the solution of the problems of the "here" and "now," a utilitarian functionalism which exalts the lived present and which effortlessly makes itself obeyed, as when we act out of a sense of routine, with a mechanical demeanor that saves us time and energy but at the same time relieves us of the effort of attention, monitoring, and criticism.

VIII

Identitarian Community

The communities will never have men in them, but only halves and quarters. They require a sacrifice of what cannot be sacrificed without detriment. The Community must always be ideal.

—*Ralph Waldo Emerson, 1842*

I saiah Berlin said that it is more stimulating to engage with ideas that are remote from, different from, and even opposed to our own than with those that resemble them, if only because acquaintance with the former helps us to keep the critical spirit alive and to be on our guard against the temptation to treat our own convictions as dogmas. This is sound advice, and especially helpful when ideas at variance with our own are endorsed by majority opinion. Of particular interest in this regard is the official website of the Movimento giovani padani, an epitome of communitarian ideology and of the

entrepreneurial ethos; a mixture, to echo Tocqueville, of egoistic individualism and communitarian identification with those
who are nearest at hand; the outcome of the stance of wishing
"to stand apart" from one's neighbors so as to separate oneself
from the "wider" society and to overcome a sense of alienation.[1]
The document in question combines a sense of the crisis of
politics as action taken in and for a wider public (founded upon
relationships of mutual trust and upon juridical ties) and a
sense of individual opportunity and economic liberalism; a
mixture of concern with technological innovations and with
the opportunities offered by the global market and also of
criticism of the condition of isolation suffered by individuals
precisely through their being absorbed by work, career, and
consumption. Marx had given this condition the name "alienation," proposing a revolutionary solution: to overturn relations
of power in order to transform the innovations of modernity
into instruments of emancipation; not so as to fall back upon
anachronistic feudal communities, but in order to realize in a
coherent fashion the promise of the Enlightenment by rendering it a possibility for everyone, a promise of the fulfillment of
individuality, nothing more and nothing less than what the
nineteenth-century liberals were proposing, albeit with different conceptual and political tools. In the perspective offered by
the Movimento giovani padani, however, the Marxist diagnosis
of alienation is employed in order to find antiuniversalist and
identitary cures to possessive individualism, whose influence,
benefits, and indeed whose logic this same movement in fact
accepts, since the community it champions has a possessive
vision of political space. Taking as its point of departure an
admission of the loss of identity, in part because of the existential and social costs imposed by the market economy, this
modern reaction to democratic individualism proposes to

recover loyalty to local identities and to ascriptive communities, confirming the diagnosis offered thirty years ago by Robert Bellah, who had maintained that individuals in liberal societies defend communitarian attachment on the grounds that it fosters sentiments of belonging and emancipates them from solitude, even though nurturing associations which reflect the qualities of the society which they are criticizing; it proposes not communities of alternative values but aggregations that are nonetheless voluntary and instrumental.[2]

According to the convincing explanation offered by Tocqueville, every society engenders its own associative forms: if in the ancien régime it was castes and corporate allegiances that provided the aggregative model consistent with the hierarchical and anti-individualist values of that social order, in a modern democracy the intermediary bodies are expressions of individualism and equality; by the same token, here the associations rest upon the voluntary decisions of subjects, who combine as equals in order to face as one their individual powerlessness to resolve specific practical questions. The communitarians think nonetheless to nurture identitary groups, which are neither provisional nor essentially "practical"; groups that in their imaginary represent and denote values specific to them alone, values that are not universalizable and hence are naturally discriminatory; finally, they think that being a member of such a group is not the outcome of an individual choice or of an imaginary and ideological creation but is instead an unrepeatable and unique fact, tied to the soil, to history, to dialect, or to the most fantastical of ancestral foundations. Although so different, both the liberals and the communitarians do nonetheless see in association with others a possible solution, in the wake of Tocqueville, to the problem of the feature whose disappearance they fear or whose revival they desire: in one case, individual autonomy, in the other, the sense of belonging.

In our consolidated and economically affluent democracies we encounter yet another phenomenon, one also apprehended by Tocqueville in the course of his American journey: identitary bonds, be they the whole country, neighborhood relationships, family, friends, or "one's own backyard," are the sites where individuals seek affective and psychological compensation for the abstract identity they have acquired through living in a society regulated by impersonal and universal norms; above all, they seek to satisfy the need, a wholly modern one, to be recognized, appreciated, and valued, all preconditions for the affirmation of individuality. The individual in our modern democracies feeds, it could be said, on "recognition," and for this reason needs to be surrounded by his fellows, by those who are part of a community of meaning and reference, and with whom it is possible to share a language, conventional signs that permit immediate communication, traditions that leave him feeling safe and protected: all tessellae of a miniature universe in which "I" can stand out from the "great" world of society, from the automatisms of the market, from the sites of mass culture, but also from the abstract identity of citizenship, the highest and most sophisticated form of political artifice and of impersonality in the relationships of respect between strangers.

It is simplistic to suppose that communitarian culture does not appreciate individual liberty, because, as Charles Taylor and Will Kymlika, among others, have observed, it is through a community of belonging that the freedom to produce and to own, to express oneself and to engage in dialogue, will unfold. The problem that arises from the new communitarian critique of democratic individualism, a critique I term "identitarian," is that it pursues a far more ambitious project: that of restricting the liberty of citizenship and civil liberties themselves to the members of the group, to those who can claim to be "brothers on a free soil," to repeat the words used on the website of the Giovani padani. Communitarians of this stripe identify themselves with a *situated* liberty, following a dualism dear to German thought on the cusp between the nineteenth and twentieth centuries, that between community and society, between gemeinschaft and gesellschaft: the first, the site of a common destiny and a storehouse of values shared and transmitted through the practice of everyday life, would designate the sphere of the virtuous and the good; the second, the site of abstract norms and rules, of obedience and of right, would for its part designate the sphere of the useful and of the just, a site where all can interact without necessarily having to know one another and to share the same cultural values, but where there is neither personalized interaction nor affective solidarity. To the first pertains the life of the community; its identity is sedimented in memory (and is kept alive through the unceasing reconstruction of memory), and it is articulated in interpersonal relationships based upon loyalty and an uncontested faith in the traditional bonds; whereas the second is an artifice of the norm, a world of relationships in which individuals are called upon to transcend their existential specificity and to regulate their relations on the basis of logics of justice.

Yet only the first of these two forms of community would seem to be capable of mobilizing individuals, and precisely because at its heart there is the dimension of duty, as distinct from the simple obligation imposed by the law, and hence it can inspire sacrifice, should the need arise. For its part, the "great" society of anonymous actors who interact through the law can at most exact obedience by way of coercion or through a calculus of costs and benefits; whatever means it may adopt, it is always in the name of an instrumental rationality and not out of a spontaneous sense of duty. The counterposing of justice and loyalty, Ota de Leonardis has written, is the guiding thread of one of the most vital mythologies "of the self-government of society," of fiduciary relationships "not mediated by the abstraction of law."[3] The reference here is to a mythology that combines laissez-faire and communitarian notions, welding together in an antistatist blend a tendency scrutinized both by sociologists of law and by social scientists, namely, the shift from relations based upon trust in the norm to relations based upon loyalty to rules and visions that are not written but shared through belonging, a phenomenon that Gunther Teubner has likened to a recrudescence of feudal identitary forms.[4] According to de Leonardis, this tendency has been exacerbated by the success of the model of New Public Management, "which asserts the superiority of managerial decisionism over the law as a source of norms that are effective, and deemed to be such, and which conversely denounces as juridification the politico-administrative regulation" dispensed by traditional politics or by the state.[5] It is the juridical culture of the law as a term of relationship independent of actors that has been seriously undermined by the myth of autonomy, be it either of economic individualism or of identitarian communitarianism.

Yet it is the "great" society, not the ascriptive society, that designates the site open to all, even to those who as members of the community may find themselves in a minority or dissenting from the majority's interpretation of the meaning of their community. To give an example that is all too topical: the immigrants who are received into "our" social-normative space as regular workers can hope to have equal respect guaranteed them far more readily in the "great" society, the one in which the politics of rights prevails, because only this society relates to them, as it does to all of us, through the instrument of the norm and according to logics of justice; whereas "our" cultural and communitarian space may prove to be far more intolerant and prone to exclude.

The paradox of the identitarian reaction to democratic individualism lies in its propensity to rehearse a new version of the possessive subject—a phenomenon that bears out the alliance observed between this communitarianism and economic liberalism. The paradox is that the community as gesellschaft may revive in other guises the dominant idea of the centrality of private ownership precisely because what has been placed in doubt within this identitary vision is the very idea of civil law, that is to say, the impersonal, abstract, and universal character of the "third person" that transcends the specific existence of those who "use" that law, that transcends the dualism of "thou" (or "you") and "I" (or "we"). In this reversal of perspective constituted by identitarian communitarianism, the impersonal and institutional dimension (the public, civil law) is, so to speak, caught, seized, and confiscated by the material dimension of ownership ("our" culture, "our" language, "our" land). The disquieting scenario implicit in this antiuniversalistic reaction consists in the fact that a material constitution, one reflecting concrete power relations (in society, in the economy, in the family, and within the "territory"), and hence indulging instead of limiting power, is superimposed upon, and in the identitarian imaginary is often substituted for, the legal or formal constitution. The law not only makes possible relationships between strangers, which is what we all are once we have stepped outside the front door, but also enhances our capacity to improve our personal and everyday world inasmuch as it forces us to train ourselves to transcend once and for all habits acquired and reinforced within our social and cultural niches, without causing us to lose all sense of our individual identities. Interacting through a "third" (the law is a transcendent self, not a negation of self) helps us in the endeavor to overcome imaginatively distances, linguistic barriers, conventions, and differences so as to be able to adopt the point of view of those who share with us the experience of life: "The individual in conversing with others is conversing also with himself and is able to call out in himself the same sort of response which he calls out in another."[6] As proof of this assertion, we may argue that the commitment of the European countries to creating a community of rules and conventions, after having massacred each other in the course of two world wars fought in close succession, was the sign of a laudable attempt of citizens who, with much mistrust and endless waverings, seek to put themselves in one another's shoes, without by any means annulling the selves that had harbored hostility, so as to attain the common ground upon which it became possible to avoid the horrors of war.

The separation of the sphere of ownership or of materiality from the sphere of impersonality and of the norm is the guarantee of the rule of law, offering security not only to noncitizens but to citizens also, because it institutes a transcendental level with respect to contingent life, thanks to which concrete individuals enter into relation or simply relate to one another and to others with respect and common decency. Without or beneath this normative level, in which individuals mirror one another, even in order to criticize their empirical circumstance or simply in order to live as equals though being in actual fact different, the civil law no longer fulfils its particular function of limiting power or of serving as a means to achieve fruitful and peaceful interaction but instead becomes a reinforced description of power, an overweening justification of it. When Joseph de Maistre said that never in his whole life had he encountered either "individuals" or "humanity" but only "Frenchmen," "Germans," or "Italians," he stripped all value from universality and transcendentality, disqualified the "as if" implicit in the law as universal (the treating of one another as equal but different), without which the specific and material immediacy of the "here" and "now" (the positive law of this or that nation) would be imposed as the sole reality, with the predictable outcome of not offering any "median term" that allows the various and multiple differences to relate one to the other in a peaceful and civil manner. In the terms of the discourse of Callicles in the *Gorgias*, it is only the world of civil law that renders possible an equal and just relation between those who are different. Conversely, through the rejection or the underestimation of the impersonal dimension, the realism of force proclaimed by Thrasymachus would return.

Undoubtedly, respecting others is not reducible to "a description of the compliance of rights such that, whenever a person does his own duty toward someone else, respect is manifested as an intrinsic and inextricable quality of the moral duty complied with."[7] The (indirect) outcome that the culture and language of rights may produce is that the individuals succeed in "being respected not out of duty" or by way of the third person (through the law; the *indirectness* of the norm) but in the "second person," or through the moral disposition of the individuals themselves, in a direct relationship to one another. But this is an acquisition or an aspiration rather than a starting point; while it would be desirable that even in the optimistic expectation that individuals come to respect each other "out of duty" they nonetheless do not give up living in a society that is based upon the impersonality of law. Furthermore, even when duty is, for the sake of argument, firmly entrenched in the minds of persons and able therefore to operate with spontaneous ease and without effort, even then one has always to counterpose to it the fact that, to echo John Locke, something may stop working, and individuals, it matters not how many or for what reason, may shatter that unity of intentions and of loyalty which seemed to render the law pointless. Yet even if one takes into account the intrinsic precariousness of moral action, it is nonetheless true that the enrichment of justice—its transformation from being an essentially normative condition to an ethical condition—is precisely what I have referred to as the culture of democratic individualism: the outcome (an aspiration rather than a definite goal) of a lengthy and laborious education of the feelings, in which, as Aristotle noted, political and social institutions, public and private life, all have a part to play.[8] One of the most important of such educational factors is indeed the language of rights, which asks of us, above all when we are faced with intractable disagreements in the second person, when, that is to say, we have to choose between the logics of right and those of community, to maintain a separation between the symbolic space represented by the norm and that represented by existence, in order to give priority to the former, to what, from antiquity onward, has assumed the name of "the rule of law," upon which the survival of the community of meaning itself ultimately depends.

Thanks to this abstract and general dimension of judgment, our empirical lives as concrete individuals, the social materiality and biographical specificity of each of us, may be reflected in the law, with the outcome not only of leading us to discriminate clearly between justice and revenge, right and power, but also of causing us to feel that beyond our immediate and historical reality, and beyond what we are in our everyday existence, there exists a wider and more general dimension in which we participate as citizens and then as human beings. Democratic individualism is transcendental in precisely this sense, because it permits communication between persons who are empirically different and strangers to one another, and thereby it enables all of us to take collective decisions relating to the questions that concern us one and all on the basis of a fundamental consent. Here we find encapsulated the emancipatory meaning of Hannah Arendt's reflection on the nature of judgment, an activity that we can perform inasmuch as we are capable of adopting an *expanded* or *general* point of view, a perspectival point of view from which we are able to understand ourselves precisely because of our capacity to transcend ourselves, knowing in the meantime that the dimension to which we are acceding is our creation, our very own creation as individuals capable of creating an order of norms: "The more people's standpoints I have present in my mind while I am pondering a given issue, and the better I can imagine how I would feel and think if I were in their place, the stronger will be my conclusion, my opinion."[9]

The problem therefore lies in the way in which we conceive of community, since it is plain that totalizing and ascriptive communities are at odds with democratic individualism, as they are with the equal right to the dignity and equality of the law. They are so for reasons of principle, as we have said, but also for sociological reasons, in the sense that they can arouse great admiration because they are capable of mobilizing individuals, inspiring a sense of sacrifice, sustaining both the aspiration toward a better society and a critique of the status quo, of an individualism that is, as we have noted, atomistic. Yet precisely because they are so demanding, such communities, notwithstanding their attractive qualities, are not destined to last long as voluntary associations and, in order to survive or to endure, are bound to become despotic or to promote conformism. Inevitably, they give rise to intolerance on the inside to the same degree as they give rise to it in relation to "others," while at the same time they discourage contact with the outside in order to avert risks of hybridization and the loosening of "intrinsic ties." Born as a sign of liberty and creativity, and reflecting the need for a rich and personalized social life, ascriptive communities end up seriously restricting the former and undermining the latter. In the manner of churches, they discourage independent thought, and they channel faith, an incalculable resource for the human will, toward the survival of the group. The free and voluntary creativity of associates is replaced by the rituality of followers, a habitual and uncritical adherence to dogmas, practices, and conventions.

Reflecting on the reasons for the collapse of the Fourierist communities that had arisen in such numbers in America in the early decades of the nineteenth century, Emerson very perceptively observed that each individual in such a community devised ingenious strategies to shield himself from the gaze of others, and to ward off inspection and idle curiosity. Faith in ourselves, the distance we manage to put between our own minds and the beliefs held by the community or enshrined in opinion, performs a hygienic function, serving not so much to protect our purportedly primordial authenticity as individuals but rather to defend our actual liberty to switch identity and opinion, to "contradict ourselves," and ultimately to permit communication between ourselves and others, dispelling the reasons for conflict. This is perhaps the most interesting dimension of the American philosophy of "self-reliance," of faith in oneself, a negative and critical dimension of surveillance of our individuality, rather than its bolstering. This, then, is why it is that the reference to receptivity becomes a reference to the value of communication between individuals and cultures, an important reference precisely in our own times, when communitarian allegiances lay claim to an authority of meaning that outstrips that of the individual conscience and impose themselves upon their members, as if they were endowed with a value that is autonomous or higher than that of the individuals of which they are composed. So far as the reification of identitary bonds is concerned, the reference to the "divinity" of each individual, and to the right each has to contradict himself in order to remain consistent with himself, it sounds like a far from anachronistic invitation to locate supremacy in reason and in character, overturning the criteria governing the selection of values, that is to say, making the person himself the fulcrum without which no community could exist. The individualist maxim of having faith in oneself serves either to *subvert* or to *regenerate* solidarity, because it functions as a tonic as regards an opaque and conformist society, and as a sedative as regards the temptation to foster self-referential and intolerant forms of communitarian belonging.

To conclude, in predemocratic societies as in the hierarchical and totalizing ones idealized by the communitarians, the individual is never alone among equals, nor is she in a relationship of reciprocity with others. She is thought of as a part of an order, caste, class, corporation, region, church, social role, and so forth. In such a universe, which is identitary and so arranged that it chooses to disregard the consent of subjects, each is assigned her place and every community is like a miniature solar system in which bodies of differing sizes gravitate around their center, searching for stability and meaning, for prescribed duties and modes of recognition as a function not of their good or of respect for their rights but first and foremost for what is good for the whole that contains them: for example, a woman will have rights as a mother and a wife, and not as a feminine person who can be, if she so wishes, a mother and a wife. As in the Ptolemaic universe, so too in the predemocratic order and in the one idealized by the identitarian communities the place of individuals is construed as a transcription of an order that was there before them and will outlive them. Alasdair MacIntyre (who, not by chance, has counterposed the Ptolemaic-Aristotelian model to the liberal, "voluntarist" one) has maintained that the identity of the individual person coincides with the recognition of a belonging, and not with a personal quest and the choice to belong, if he wishes it. Individual identity here implies a narrative of the whole community, a narrative that is in its turn presumed to be unitary, just as a "total harmonious scheme of human life" is.[10] Such a circumstance is alien to democratic culture because it prescribes a way of life that may be intolerant of individual choices, and therefore at odds with the pluralism of values and with rights themselves. Not by chance Tocqueville was at pains to argue that democratic society was an alternative, above all else, to aristocratic society: "Aristocracy links everybody, from peasant to king, in one long chain. Democracy breaks the chain and frees each link."[11] Equality it was that broke the chain of inegalitarian relationships and of dependency, and equality likewise necessarily gave rise to the principle of the "sovereignty of individual judgment": upon both rests the idea of the deliberating collective, of the citizens who autonomously decide what to deliberate and decide upon, and following which rules. As we anticipated in chapter 1, the meaning and value of democracy derives from an awareness of the limited nature of each citizen and of the possibility of correcting that limited nature through association and cooperation with others, combining the diverse capacities for a purpose that is useful to one and all. Thus there cannot be an identitarian democracy any more than there can be an authoritarian democracy, for in either case it would be an oxymoron in which the idea of government by means of the free expression of opinions is confused with that of the consent of the numerically and ideologically preponderant part.

IX

Regeneration

This is why, whereas in the ordinary classification of the rights of liberty, civil liberties are distinguished from political liberties (the rights of man *from those of the* citizen*), I prefer to consider here all the rights that are designed to protect the independence of the single individual within his own sphere, in terms of their* altruistic *function, and to number them all among the* political *liberties. The rights of liberty must not in fact be conceived, in a democratic regime, as the barbed wire enclosure within which the single individual seeks refuge from the assaults of a hostile community, but rather as the door that enables him to go out from his little garden into the street, and to bring from there his contribution to the common endeavor: liberty, that is, not as a guarantee of selfish isolation but as a guarantee of social expansion. Where these rights are suppressed, there truly, as if to hide from the encroaching oppression of authority,*

*the individual retreats into himself and loses his sense of
collective solidarity.*

—*Piero Calamandrei, 1946*

In both the old and the new critiques of individualism,
which frequently intersect with the critiques of modernity, there is often a mistrust of the dimension of research
or of experiment, a state of mutability and subjectivism
that has been held to blame for the relativist character of
moral life in the democracies and, ultimately, for the subversion
of every anchorage of the duty that transcends individual
evaluation.[1] Charles Taylor has accused the universalist politics
of democratic liberalism of tacitly presupposing an individualist metaphysics, despite the fact that the individual postulated
by democratic society is not utilitarian and "possessive" but
endowed with a sense of justice that, as may be seen from
Piero Calamandrei's words quoted above, renders him capable
of formulating political judgments that are not unconcerned
with personal interest, although inspired by criteria of impar-
tiality and universality.[2] The just society of constitutional
democracy rests upon principles to which everyone would in
theory be disposed to subscribe because they guarantee a
politics of dignity precisely when they deny to anyone whatsoever—even if an elected majority—the right to correct the
beliefs of someone and to impose his own as true. Rights, as
Norberto Bobbio has reminded us, are not a resetting to zero
of differences but rather are modes and criteria of relationship
through which attention to differences can coherently coexist
with the form of democratic life.[3]

It is equality that transmits this perennial movement to
the social process, that allows the "ought to be" in politics without binding politics to any particular realization save for those
which from time to time seem best to honor its promise. Carlo
Rosselli had very perceptively observed that democracy is the
only regime which does not have a specific goal and which is a
perpetual movement toward an end that is always beyond its
contingent realizations. "Among democratic peoples," Tocqueville concluded, "men easily obtain a certain equality, but
they will never get the sort of equality they long for. . . . Every
instant they think they will catch it, and each time it slips
through their fingers."⁴ The dimension of the imaginary (as
opposed to what is descriptive), while it protects equality from
its potentially tyrannical degenerations—for example, sameness
or when we identify with the specific mode of being of a group
of our fellows—releases democracy from any specific social
goal to be actualized. Endogenous mutability is the term that
best describes a political order in which no one has the competence and the power to give a definitive answer to any public
question; in which the rule of the majority represents the preventative admission, the taking into account of the fact that for
every decision taken there could always be a different answer,
and every solution deemed good today could tomorrow appear
inadequate or in need of revision. Because of this condition,
which admits at one and the same time fallibility and perfect-
ibility, individual rights perform their function of guarantee
and clamp upon the constituted power and upon the future
pretensions of that power; they are never absolute, because they
presume an individual life that unfolds with others, in a reciprocity of requests and obligations. They describe a condition
of collaboration and research. Cesare Pavese had noted as much
in his commentary upon the 1931 Spoon River anthology. He

had ventured to interpret the "dead" of Edgar Lee Masters through those of Dante, only all of a sudden to abandon the attempt: "Since Dante's dead have a universal schema of which they are a part, and none of the damned would dream of criticizing their destination, whereas those of Spoon River, even when dead, have not found an answer. . . . This is the essentially modern poem, one of research, and of the insufficiency of every schema, of need at once individual and collective."[5]

This brief discussion furnishes us with some idea of the complexity of democracy, the name as much of an institutional order as of a way of conceiving of politics and participation in society. It denotes a reality that we have never fully experienced, even if over the centuries we have perfected it so far as institutions and rules are concerned, and gradually accepted it as the most desirable of governments. This structural incompletion emanates from the two fundamental values that characterize democracy, namely, equality and individual autonomy; the idea, that is, that human beings, women and men alike, are equal in value and moral dignity and that no one has by nature, tradition, convention, and human or divine will a higher power by virtue of which she can take decisions bearing upon the lives of others without or against their consent. As Piero Calamandrei convincingly explains in the epigraph to the present chapter,[6] individualism as a democratic ideal is not only not to be identified with egoism but in addition represents a powerful challenge to communitarian "perfectionism," itself a collective form of egoism; moreover, it amounts to a denunciation of the obsession with identitary assimilation as a condition of the good life for the individual and society alike; and a denunciation, finally, of the identification of trust with loyalty to a given code of values. The epithet "transcendental" that American nineteenth-century romantics began to affix to the term "individuality" hinges upon this complex notion of individual specificity and trust in oneself, ethical and psychological conditions that allow persons to maintain a critical distance from their specific and contingent possessions, identifications, and modes of fulfillment so as to relate to their milieu "not under a personal but under a universal light."[7] It is this yearning to transcend empirical existence without neglecting the specific condition of persons that inspires education for equality and the inclusive and tolerant nature of democracy. We are not concerned here with a spontaneous process or with a characteristic that emerges directly and simply through an act of contractual decision making; rather, it is an ethical factor, the outcome of an educative process to which democratic procedures contribute indirectly, habituating persons to accepting the provisionality of decisions, the ideas of others, and free debate; or to taking into account the possibility of changing one's ideas and even of admitting publicly that one is mistaken. Dialogue between equals rests upon respect for autonomy of judgment and upon reciprocity: the supplying of reasons for what one is proposing or opposing is a mark of respect for others and a commitment to endeavoring to be public actors, not merely private individuals.

These practices of democratic interaction require support from the educational system and the overall organization of private and social life, such as the family and the workplace. Since the eighteenth century, the history of democratization in the West has been a complex tale of the transformation of society and of the economy, not only of government, demonstrating that there cannot be a "good democracy" if one and the same person enjoys rights as a citizen but lives a considerable part of his private life in relationships of subordination or command. It is hard for political democracy to subsist and to remain

secure when the social order is structured according to forms
of power in which authority has no limits save the self-interest
or good will of those who are exercising it. As theorists and
militants of suffragism would acknowledge (supplying the
politics of the social question and of labor with important
questions), if it is true that practical action in everyday life is a
school for social feelings, then it is likewise the case that polities
needing to train up citizens cannot tolerate families that train
up masters and slaves, nor a society that justifies practices that
offend, or entail the moral abuse of, women. The "atmosphere"
of liberty that the democratic transformation of society creates
enters into house and home and radically alters private relationships between men and women, and between adults and children; it enters into the workplace so as to subordinate the
domination of property and command to the principle of the
dignity of the person and to the principle of the guarantees of
liberty. Social scientists have given the name "social capital" to
this set of variables that mold behaviors but cannot be "measured" or "touched," even though not only the robustness of
the rule of law but actual economic performance depends upon
their intangible presence in the everyday life of a community.[8]
In this sense, as we shall see in the final chapter, the distinction
between public and private is very far from being a simple and
accomplished fact, precisely because the principle of respect for
persons is a foundation that politics shares with ethics, becoming the central element in the atmosphere of liberty that con-
stitutes the "cement" of modern society.

Indubitably, if the form of government is not the only
aspect of public and social interaction to which the term
"democracy" may be applied, it is because there is implicit in
the constitution of the democratic state a reference to a good
that is metajuridical: the single person or individual, a good

which should never be placed in question and which the institutions are called upon to protect, thereby helping to promote
directly or indirectly social relationships that serve in their turn
to foster respect; this relation between the inside and the outside
of the institutions ensures that these latter are able to reproduce
themselves while at the same time they train subjects in their
everyday relationships to embrace the norms of common decency and to apply them without strain. It follows that the
democratic constitution is something more than a piece of
paper; it presupposes and fosters a cultural and moral loyalty,
a "feeling of allegiance" that the procedures, rules, and institutions are supposed to translate into a guide to conduct in all
social relationships. In its turn, and as if it were in a circular
relationship, the force of this metajuridical ethos is transmitted
to the social body as a whole, to public and private relationships,
fostering that atmosphere of liberty and respect invoked above.
The sovereignty of individual judgment—the same principle
as justifies "government by means of discussion"—is the "fixed
point" (what the citizens agree to regard as "sacred") that holds
democratic society together, that which by common acknowledgment is placed beyond discussion and disagreement and
without which disagreement and decisions according to the
rule of the majority cannot be entertained.

   We are concerned here not simply with a principle of
private morality but with a value that gives to democracy its
ethical specificity, making of it a political order that manages
to ground its own stability precisely upon the uncertainty this
principle entails, opening itself up to the contribution of citizens, adopting, as we anticipated in chapter 1, an inclusive and
cooperative strategy. Trust, upon which the relationship of
cooperation between those who are equal and different is
founded, is a predicate of cognitive incompletion, and a mark,

at one and the same time, of uncertainty and of having the resource to collaborate. "In conditions of certainty—either when there is complete knowledge of the behavior of others or when, conversely, there is blind faith—there is no need for trust. Calculation or submission will suffice."[9] This renders democratic cooperative action different both from that modeled upon economic individualism (*homo oeconomicus*) and from that modeled upon religious individualism, though it borrows from the one the centrality for the subject of self-interest, and from the other the prop of belief. We shall now endeavor to grasp the comprehensive nature of the culture of democratic transcendental individuality.

Albert Hirschman has written that the victory of the liberal and democratic solution can be read as the final outcome of the long process of transition from militarist to commercial society, from the values of heroism and of the forceful virtues of the citizen-soldier to the prosaic and private ones of tranquillity and of looking out for oneself, of substituting for exceptionality and chance a civil existence of *routine* and of everyday normality where public duties (from the paying of taxes to voting) are distributed with periodical regularity and in such a fashion as to allow citizens to include them among their ordinary tasks and to minimize the sacrifice involved.[10] Max Weber called this docile submission to regulated habit the fruit of "legal-rational authority," a form of social discipline that is intense and interiorized (intense because interiorized), and that is rooted in the individual conscience, hinging precisely upon self-interest, without any recourse to a direct and permanent indoctrination. Classical heroism is too costly a good for the modern individual, who, Constant said, prefers tranquillity and calculated enterprise to the expressive singularity of the exemplary endeavor. There is no greater virtue, Emerson wrote, than work and the industrious life: "All honest men are daily striving to earn their bread by their industry . . . and constitutions and governments exist for that,—to protect and insure it to the laborer."[11] These characteristics, which are both normative and part and parcel of ordinary morality, render democratic citizenship different from both the republican and the liberal forms; it reinterprets the former's notion of civics, and the latter's separation of spheres of life. By contrast with the republican form of citizenship, the democratic form proves to be far less ostentatious and dogmatic. The republican idea of citizenship and of politics is theoretically selective and nonegalitarian, inasmuch as it makes demands upon citizenship and upon individual capacities; certainly, it calls for something more than mere obedience and the capacity to formulate moral judgments. Perhaps it was for this reason that Rousseau, an egalitarian republican, had imposed silence upon the citizens gathered together in an assembly, since the use of speech, which is associated with inequality in competence, may give rise to perverse effects such as the manipulation of consent on the part of orators promoting particular interests, or cause the reason of citizens to stray far from the public good. Setting aside any evaluation of his identification of political legitimacy with direct participation, it is evident that in wishing to include everyone in the sovereign body, Rousseau had correctly foreseen that one could impose neither the prerequisite of competence or knowledge nor that of virtue. For inclusion in the sovereign body it was and ought to be sufficient that the citizens were all normally capable of formulating moral arguments and of understanding their own self-interest (of knowing how to argue in terms of the just and the useful, a function that, precisely on account of the natural feelings of self-love and empathy toward others, everyone was capable of performing). Recognizing the just and the misguided, for Rousseau as for the other theorists of the age, came easily enough to everyone thanks to the natural reasonableness all had in common (on the basis of this same premise Montesquieu had maintained that, while it was not appropriate for everyone to take part directly in deciding the laws, it was desirable that all participate in the choice of representatives, since, though not competent to decide upon specific questions, they were, however, naturally capable of distinguishing the just from the unjust and hence of evaluating men and their behavior, if correctly informed). There is a modicum of "truth" in the opinion of the democrats that the assembly has a central role to play in the state, for whereas single individuals may fall into error when it is a question of deliberating on arguments that concern the collectivity, "whenever they are gathered together" they can put to good use the "virtues" and "wisdoms" that are scattered to differing degrees among all of them. Individuals who are limited and imperfect, and not excelling in intelligence and knowledge, "when they are brought together, just as in the mass they become as it were one man with many pairs of feet and hands and many senses, so also do they become one in regard to character and intelligence."[12]

In essence, to be included in sovereignty does not require one either to possess a definite quantity of virtue (how much?) or of knowledge (of or about what?), or to undergo any particular apprenticeship (learned from whom?), nor to have any qualification beyond the mere fact of existing. In concluding his reflections against slavery and the exclusion of women from public life, the Marquis de Condorcet elaborated the following two maxims freighted with political implications: the human species is one and does not contain inferior and superior races within it; human beings are all equal, aside from the qualities (natural and social) that distinguish them one from another, since they all have the capacity to make and change previously made decisions and ideas, and above all to suffer, to perceive the sufferings of others, to defend their own lives, and to avert the causes of suffering. For this reason, reducing a man to slavery or making a woman into a domestic servant were for Condorcet "crimes" pure and simple, as it also was a crime to tolerate the existence of laws or behaviors that rendered such things possible.[13] Is the politics of virtue a necessary condition for establishing a correspondence between laws and institutions on the one hand and these same principles on the other? Condorcet counseled suspicion of the politics of virtue, because it confused trust with faith, or the uncertainty that the former implied with the overcoming of uncertainty that the latter entailed; it conceived of institutions as coercive agents that imposed good conduct rather than as organizations of conduct that trusted to individual self-interest in well-being in order to stimulate virtuous conduct.

Yet citizenship as civil religion is excessively demanding: it imposes obligations that are not solely moral, it assigns to the state a direct ethical and educative function, and it calls upon everyone to make an active commitment to the fatherland and to cultivate a profound sense of communitarian identity and of belonging, which, precisely on account of its ethical and civic richness, may foster exclusion or fail to be open and receptive. Even when, as in contemporary theoretical republicanism, one tends to give prominence to procedures and to the constitution, to the rules for monitoring power and protecting liberty, references to virtue and to the direct formation of the virtuous character are not wholly abandoned, and are actually implied. Republican citizenship is a mixture of rules and procedures, and of good customs and civic virtue.[14] In order to obviate this identitary limit ingrained in republican civism,

Habermas has sought to confine patriotism to constitutional-
ism, to the shared support of the norms for a reason at once
self-interested and civic, since they are bound by a double thread
to the world of interests and to that of the law, at one and the
same time regulating the private and building up the public.
The transcription into politics of the civism of "self-interest
properly understood," to use one of Tocqueville's most felicitous
expressions, is an example often applied in works of contemporary sociopolitical research where they seek to go beyond the
element of passion contained within classical republicanism
through the institutionalization of fiduciary relationships, the
"civilizing" routine of associative practices.[15]

Political action in democracy has an ineradicably
voluntary character that cannot be assimilated by a virtue
transmuted into habit and routine. The voluntary nature of
participation, while it does not guarantee the efficacy of civism
in the political choices made by citizens, does nonetheless indicate just how hospitable democracy is toward individuals,
since it is not perfectionist in judging their capacities and character. Let us recall, to give just one example, the fact that when
in Periclean Athens the absenteeism of citizens threatened to
undermine the functioning of the institutions, it was decided
to pay with funds from the treasury the equivalent of a day's
labor to anyone willing to attend an assembly or to serve on the
popular juries. Implicit in this decision were two important
assumptions, namely, that democratic citizens are persons who
live by their labor, and participation may therefore be particularly demanding and costly; and that, even when requested,
participation is nonetheless not a duty or a service dissociated
from individual interest and from voluntary decision making.
This has two consequences: in the first place, political functions
in a democracy must be remunerated because participation is

an activity that is not part of the *otium* of those not obliged to live off their own labor; in the second place, the offering of an incentive to participate, as against legal obligation or duty, is more consistent with the presumption that participation is voluntary. The indirect way chosen by Athens, which used an economic incentive to dissuade citizens from abstaining but did not impose participation, was consistent with the principle of the sovereignty of individual judgment and equality of opportunity in political participation and equality of treatment by civil law (*isonomia* and *isegoria*).[16]

Finally, democratic politics, by contrast with the republican form, is anyway not a politics of virtue, if by virtue we mean, as republicans assuredly do, a politics in which participation serves to limit and contain the private dimension of interests (republican virtue is sustained by a dualism between a world of individual self-interest and a world of public duty—between individual and citizen).[17] It is interesting to observe in this regard that although Montesquieu had included democracy among the republican forms, thereby aligning it with the spirit of "virtue," he had nonetheless recognized that Athens had some difficulty in sustaining the republican spirit, precisely on account of the individualistic nature of its society, and ultimately he had specified that the democratic "virtue" par excellence is equality, a virtue in itself individualistic because it induces each to monitor the position of others (so as to avert the ever-present possibility of privileges arising) and the law (in relation to the position each of them has in society). One could indeed add that the republican idea of citizenship denotes a vision of politics which is critical of democracy, because mistrustful of equality in consideration, and of legitimacy arrived at through majority decisions and above all proverbially suspicious of an institutional order founded upon consent rather than upon virtue and competence. Furthermore, as the historians know full well, republicanism (which owes its conceptual and institutional identity to Rome, not to Athens) has been construed as a response not only to monarchy but also to popular government, deemed no less than the monarchical a bad or degenerate form of government.[18] It is this that we learn from classical and modern republicans: from Cicero to Polybius, as also from James Harrington and John Milton. Republican dissatisfaction with government by number is still to be found in the writings of a republican theorist like Philip Pettit, who, though mistrustful of the classical politics of virtue, is nevertheless careful to oppose the "republic of reason" (the virtue of the moderns, it might be called) to government by "popular will" or by passion (it does not matter whether through parliaments or through referenda), and therefore suggests that we "depoliticize democracy" in order to render decisions less exposed to the will of assemblies and to partisan struggles, whether by extending the juridical sphere to the detriment of the political or by giving more scope to consultation of those with competence and of commissions of experts.[19]

In conclusion, republican citizenship is not of sufficient help to us in our attempts to understand democratic citizenship, if only because it does not manifest the same sensitivity toward the egalitarian foundations of politics—where by "egalitarian" I mean the spirit of equal respect (in law but also in ordinary morality) for all human beings, irrespective of the nature of their contribution to the political community, or of the degree of their conformity to shared values. The nobility that will adapt best to the democratic *common person* is the one that displays "a new respect for the sacredness of the individual" person in her or his concrete existence; this is the only effective "antidote" able to correct a "disgraceful deference to public opinion" and to the constituted power.[20] The virtue of courage does not fade, therefore, but is transformed and becomes an assertion of one's own sovereignty of judgment and of one's own responsibility; the courage to differ, to not yield to the majority opinion precisely when one is helping to shape it. As we shall see in the next chapter, the most distinctive democratic virtue is that of dissent.

Democratic loyalty takes its measure from the manner in which the antiheroic heroism of everyday life is evaluated. If you want our nation to pursue greatness, and its citizens to cultivate "heroic virtues" rather than "calm habits," Tocqueville wrote, with a hint of nostalgia for the aristocratic past, democracy is not the regime for you. This was not the neutral observation of a social scientist but the resigned acknowledgment of one who despite himself was having to come to terms with the fact that the age of "glory" and of a "brilliant society" was in its twilight years.[21] In *Politics*, Emerson defined moral equality as the foundation of democratic government, and distinguished the rights of the person from the rights of property in order to say that individuals, though unequal in their enjoyment of these latter, "all have equal rights, in virtue of being identical in nature ... in virtue of their access to reason."[22] Emerson did what Tocqueville found it hard to do: in order to separate the individual from equality of social condition he bound him to equality of value, a value that rested not upon the pursuit of honors and upon civic service to the community but upon the simple moral recognition of his own dignity and that of others, a dignity stemming from living as associates under democratic laws. Yet is acceptance of the other the same thing as indifference? Or, conversely, is it the same thing as sharing and uniformity? The manner in which we formulate these questions should help us to clarify the other pole of difference in relation to which we can appreciate the specificity of democratic citizenship, namely, liberal citizenship. If in the case of republicanism the term of comparison is the quality of participation, in this case it is the interpretation of tolerance, or what it is one understands by acceptance of, and respect for, the other.

The receptive and sympathetic individuality that democracy fosters does something more (and better) than simply accepting the fact that others are as they are, so long as they remain on the margins of our own life, so long as they do not undermine our certainties and interfere with our liberty to be what we choose and wish to be, so long as they live their difference in silence, in the privacy of their consciences and their peripheries, and in the shadow zone of minority opinions. Liberal tolerance cannot, without further adjustments, be counted among the moral virtues of the democratic citizen, since "in order for there to be tolerance . . ., one must as a preliminary prefer the nonexistence or disappearance of the difference" to be tolerated.[23] It neither requires nor implies a dialogical relationship, and it does not presuppose a notion of equality as respect on account of which "each instantaneously can judge the feelings of all the others; he just casts a rapid glance at himself, and that is enough."[24] "In all people I see myself . . .," declared Walt Whitman. "And the good or bad I say of myself I say of them."[25] This is why, as Tocqueville observed, there is no misery that the democratic individual "cannot readily understand, and a secret instinct tells him its extent. It makes no difference if strangers or enemies are in question; his imagination at once puts him in their place."[26] This account tallies with what Gustavo Zagrebelsky has recently written about the extent, and limits, of respect. "But self-respect is not enough; one also needs respect, in others, of the same dignity that we recognize in ourselves. . . . In actual fact simple respect of oneself and contempt for others leads not to democracy but to the affirmation of one's own autocracy, with the aim of avoiding the need for, and the limitation upon, a necessary reciprocal coordination."[27]

Liberal tolerance, the sort that rests upon the argument from prudence and that historically arose through the sixteenth- and seventeenth-century wars for identitary recognition, particularly of the religious kind, corresponds to peace through armistice—"on account of exhaustion"—and is built upon "a scene of ruins" and the failure of accords.[28] It reveals, at bottom, an attitude that, as Thomas Paine suggested, consists in allowing the mad the liberty to believe, if they so wish, in absolute monarchy or in any other folly that departs from the "truth," such as "taking the ass for the lion," provided that "I do not imitate their humility, nor disturb their devotions"; provided that they do not disturb mine or interfere in my beliefs.[29] The premise that justifies liberal tolerance, and that may be traced back to John Locke and Baruch Spinoza, is the clear separation between theoretical and practical activity, between affairs that pertain to the civil authority (first and foremost, peace) and those that pertain to faith and to faith communities. For the classical liberals, who lived in a post-Reformation Europe still hostile to religious pluralism, the problem was principally that of guaranteeing everyone the right to profess their own faith or their own philosophy without interference from the civil power or from other faiths. Consequently, they argued that this liberty had to be granted without restriction in the inner space of the conscience but not without restriction in the outer space of civil life (to Locke social peace entailed tolerating neither Catholics nor atheists).[30] Their fundamental conviction was that one could distinguish with analytic simplicity between interiority and exteriority, between intellectual activity and practical activity. In all probability, it was the romantic turn and the new attention paid to individual expressivity that allowed thinkers to complicate the habitual dualism and to open up a path going beyond liberal tolerance. No matter how freedom of thought and conscience is affirmed or denied for the members of one's own group and for others, whether one assumes a dogmatic stance toward the bearers of other beliefs (describing them as falsehoods or prejudices) or whether in the end one favors skepticism and a prudential stance toward all confessions in general, the fact remains that in every case one presupposes the existence of others, with their beliefs and their dogmatic or skeptical truths, with their unpleasant habits and even their insufferable choices. "All of that sheds light upon the precariousness of the resolution and answer suggested by the prudential argument" and upon the complicated resolution of the public/private division.[31] Complicated because the divergence between beliefs and identity, or the conflict, can be a cause of stability only when it rests upon a common acceptance (out of conviction) of the foundations of collective life.

Haughty tolerance of the mad who take "the ass for the lion" or prudent acceptance of them in their apathy, and of all such folly, is not perfectly adapted to democratic individuality, even if it is its necessary premise—as it has been historically and can still be today, precisely on account of a disturbing revival of identitary politics, in relation to which liberal tolerance acquires a renewed urgency and topicality. But equality as a value, the feeling of sympathy, curiosity itself toward what is different—perhaps to criticize it, or to welcome it, and often to imitate it—impels one beyond liberal tolerance, in the direction of dialogue and a readiness to listen. "In order to arrive at dialogue," Guido Calogero observed, "one must not only 'tolerate' or 'admit' other visions of things, one must feel a genuine curiosity about them."[32] One must be intent upon understanding "other mental worlds," and prepared not to exclude one's own world from critical comparison; in other words, one must adopt a stance that is Socratic in nature, not Platonist (doctrinaire) or Sophist (indifferent or instrumental). Not even the pugnacious spirit of the Enlightenment Voltairian, prepared to fight to the death against another's opinions while at the same time defending with equal intransigence his or her right to hold them, is in reality much inclined to dialogue or free of dogmatism, because a responsive and dialogical disposition excludes "a prophecy that will never in any circumstance accept an interlocutor's thesis. . . . One cannot constantly fight for another's freedom of thought if one is not also at the same time interested in its possible content," if one does not also take into account the possibility of being converted. The distance between liberal toleration and dialogical availability once again confirms the more-than-tolerant character of democratic civil life and its rootedness in an authentic ethical principle—respect for another's dignity and liberty—which at the same time becomes a political custom. The rules of democracy are born of moral conscience, because "it is precisely moral conscience that tells me not to believe ever that I am right beyond a shadow of a doubt, and not to expect others to give me a fair hearing, if first of all I am not capable of giving them a fair hearing."[33]

The question that arises at this point has to do with the form assumed by dissent, or even by an explicit voicing of disgust for another's stance or style of life. If, as Whitman has so aptly written, democracy is the kingdom of the beautiful and of the ugly, this does not mean a suspension of judgment, not least because the ugly and the beautiful must all the same be recognized and described as such. To say that an individual is capable of empathy and sympathy, and that he succeeds in adopting impartial reasons when judging, does not entail thinking of him as a being who does not express moral judgments or suspends his judgments as to how his fellows live in order not to unsettle sympathy with disagreement. The question is relative then to the forms that intolerance may assume in a society that promotes pluralism precisely because it is individualist. Respect for others does not imply that we do not express or cannot publicly express our moral judgment upon their ideas or their life choices. The expressing of a judgment of disapproval is an act of liberty that nonetheless must not lead to—ought not to lead to—a mobilization against the person who is the object of the disapproval. As Mill had sensed, the forms of moral disagreement are the question upon which tolerance plays in modern democracies. For whereas political disagreement is regulated by constitutional procedures, and religious disagreement has found correspondences in the charters of rights, moral disagreement, for its part, rests essentially upon the self-limitation that each individual must impose upon her own attitudes and feelings, and in the last analysis upon her own language. Each of us must learn how to disagree or disapprove without translating our judgments into expressions of intolerance or discrimination.

As we saw in chapter 3, the romantic conception to which democratic individualism is indebted entails the interpretation of individual experience as a complex event that sets in motion faculties of various different kinds such as the emotions, the intellect, and the passions, memory, and reason. The human liberty that is consolidated through individual rights is not exhausted by the claim to brook no interference from the law but in addition unfolds as "expressivity": putting these rights into practice means that each can choose to live as she wishes so long as she does not cause any harm to others or prevent others from living as they would wish. Under the heading of

free expression we ought also to include the liberty to adopt
ways or styles of life, and not only that of having ideas or expressing opinions; a liberty with respect not only to the laws of
the state but also with regard to the opinions of others and of
the majority, to the culture at large and to consolidated habits.
This is an aspect of the utmost importance because it indicates
that when one speaks of tolerance in democratic societies one
should presume not that individual actions (or those actions
that regard individuals) are "pragmatically performed behind
closed doors," or without external interference, but that they
are instead openly carried out before others, in civil society, and
therefore exposed to others' reactions, to the interference of the
judgment of others.[34] Admittedly, the law is indeed the first
source of coercion and limitation of liberty; yet judgment and
opinion can likewise elicit obedience and be intrusive, although
they do not have at their disposal the same coercive instruments
as the law does. And since individual liberty is expressivity, styles
of life and the moral values that such styles represent necessarily become an object of public debate—with the potential risks
to individual liberty that this entails—even when they do not
violate any law or are not in conflict with the law.

The principle of noninterference on the part of the law
therefore does not exhaust the notion of individual liberty in
a democracy precisely because it does not account for the difference between tolerance (an attitude that is negative or that
entails self-control) and respect or acceptance of others (an
attitude that is positive or that is an overt expression of judgment), and because it does not take into consideration those
forms of interference that operate indirectly and by way of
opinion. Liberty as noninterference cannot be said to guarantee
individual liberty in a satisfactory manner if it means, for example, that a person is free to express his homosexuality only

in the privacy of his heart and in the secrecy of his house in order not to suffer the rebuke of others' opinions. This would not be tolerance but be the enforced privatization of a form of conduct that the opinion of the majority rejects and censures, even if it is not censured by the laws and by law. In this scenario, tolerance would assume the guise of not according visibility to forms of conduct that general opinion despises and hates; it would assume the guise of an effective limitation upon the individual expression of liberty. Individual freedom of opinion and of feelings in all contexts, moral or speculative, is therefore found to be at variance with the traditional notion of liberal tolerance as a practice that confines to privacy whatever the morality of the majority does not endorse.[35] The expression of individual liberty in a society founded upon equality of respect involves the existence and the manifestation of differences in opinion and in styles of life (that is, of values). This perspective entails a redefinition of classical liberalism and of the distinction between public and private implicit in it.

A revisiting of Mill may help us to understand the relevance of this redefinition, because he was one of the first theorists to propose an idea of the public that embraces both the political sphere or sphere of sanction (in which legal judgment operates) and the social sphere or sphere of persuasion (in which evaluative moral judgment operates and sanction is only indirect, operating through dissuasion against a particular form of conduct or through action upon passions such as shame and the fear of being excluded). "Public" means not only the state but also the sphere intermediate between the state and the inner world of the feelings (the private world par excellence). From the state's point of view, this intermediate sphere of liberty defines an area that is one of indifference (liberty extends up to the point at which the law does not intervene). Yet from the point of view of evaluative social judgment, the public sphere may become the site of a new form of coercion—the one that uses "moral" means to induce uniformity of conduct, such as manipulation and stigmatization. Foucault showed very convincingly how control of the mind and of our most intimate feelings is the strategy that civil society employs to marginalize styles of life that do not conform to ordinary morality, and without using the coercion of the law, in order to repress, that is to say, individuality in its uniqueness.

It can therefore be said that just as constitutional guarantees are a bulwark against the coercion of political decisions (and "the main objective of those who love liberty"), by the same token the critical ethos (the propensity to ask for reasons, to consult, to seek to understand) is a bulwark against the coercive power of the "public in general." This model is inspired by the role played by Socrates in Athens, who encountered his interlocutors in the guise of moral individuals (private persons) in the public space of the city, yet engaged them in dialogue in an open form that defied conventional and traditional wisdom by appealing to the authority of the individual conscience.

Idealistic though it may be, this vision of democratic individuality aspires to extend the communicative dimension beyond the sphere of politics and the state, into the so-called private dimension, without, however, losing its public nature. We are concerned here with a perspective in some ways akin to that proposed more recently by Hannah Arendt. In a democratic society, the dimension of the "public" is expanded beyond the state and the political sphere to embrace personal social relations and styles of life, actual familial and sexual relationships, private forms that in an open society of the kind to be found in a democracy are exposed to the public or foster modes of conduct that have an impact upon public judgment. It is within this extended conception of the "public" that we should locate democratic individuality; a specification that implies an essentially communicative perspective, and therefore one that is fatally exposed to interference on the part of current opinion and, conversely, to agonistic confrontation.

Now, this conception of public life and of critical respect cannot be equated with a neutral or agnostic liberalism, since it presumes that government plays an active role both in establishing the circumstances for the development of the individual and in guaranteeing pluralism and the practice of respect.[36] We are concerned with a democratic liberalism, therefore, which distinguishes very clearly between opportunities that are external or written in the rules and the personal commitment of the individual to using and making the most of them. Where this latter commitment is concerned, the state is supposed to remain neutral or to abstain from intervening, since it cannot impose upon any citizen a vision of the good life and hence one type of commitment as against another without prejudicing fundamental liberties. Democratic individuals "are not to be blamed for not being saintly or heroic," and any punishment the state imposes upon them is not with a view to shaping their character or beliefs.[37] Mill "does not doubt that some beliefs are genuinely truer than others, but he rules out in the same essay [*On Liberty*] any intervention by the state with the object of moulding character or belief."[38] This criterion contains the most radical rebuttal both of identitarian individualism and of possessive individualism, and indeed of the ethical conception of the state, that is, of entrusting the state with the task of shaping individual and social morality.

The problem of the difficult, if not intractable relationship between truth and power, was brought to light with exceptional shrewdness by Hume and Condorcet, who each addressed it without eliminating the dichotomy between the supremacy of the will (political power) and the supremacy of knowledge (truth). Even if humanity as a whole were to assert with conviction that the sun moves around the earth and that this latter is fixed at the center of the universe, Hume observed, even in this case such a conviction would not cease to be mistaken. On the basis of these same premises, Condorcet explored in his studies on elections the possibility of closing the gap between truth and voting, without, however, entertaining the possibility of equating the two. In order to resolve the dichotomy, or better still in order to do so in such a way that it did not lead to undesirable or wayward solutions, Condorcet looked beyond the matter of procedures: he advocated a plan of national education, assigning to the state the task, not of pursuing the truth or of inducing citizens to pursue it, but rather of so arranging matters that citizens might be able to resolve the contradiction between power and truth when it presented itself. A government might be reckoned good if it did not resist the spread of knowledge, indeed if it facilitated it by all means possible (whether by instituting a national system of education, or by allowing absolute freedom to science and to the circulation of ideas), although its role stopped there, since political power could not teach the right choices or cultivate claims to being inherently ethical, inasmuch as progress toward the truth has to do with knowledge and not with will—it is a cognitive question, not a question of power. The state should therefore "arm itself against error," yet not by imposing the truth but rather by rendering citizens capable of seeking it, of seeing, therefore, and of correcting error. The objective of the democratic state was to advance knowledge, not to establish the truth.[39] Two opposed risks emerge from this surprising conclusion to Condorcet's inquiry, one arising from the ethical state and the other from scientism.

In specifying the nature of these two risks we should be able to clarify the question of the limits upon the neutrality of the democratic state, or specify just what it is that it cannot tolerate.

Democratic liberalism is both a culture and ideology and a theory of the institutional techniques required to limit political power and to enable the organs of the state to deliver impartial justice. This renders the meaning, use, and extension of neutrality a problem to which unambiguous solutions cannot readily be supplied. In order to make room for pluralism, constitutional democracy does not need to combine procedural neutrality with a moral philosophy of neutrality.[40] What democratic theorists are now proposing is a distinction between the political dimension of ideologies or of ideas and the institutional or legal dimension. We require public servants and magistrates to maintain a "position of critical distance" with regard to political visions, be they their own or those of the majority, but we cannot ask as much of citizens, nor indeed of their representatives. Assigning to liberalism a status *super partes* implies the belief that there is an equivalence between the level of ideas and that of institutions and procedures, between the level of politics and that of the law. Yet where the legal order is concerned, neutrality means protecting norms from partisan designs and intentions which arise in the sphere of interpretation, and which, if transposed directly into the state, could well foster intolerance and place the equal treatment of citizens and the actual stability of society at risk. Nonetheless, while this attitude of neutrality is reasonable when applied to certain ethical conceptions, it is not absolutely so, since, as we have several times observed, at the basis of democratic society there is in fact the fundamental value or good we know as the individual.

One can reasonably ask whether neutrality should be applied equally and indiscriminately to religions and to the

concrete opportunities individuals need in order to realize their
life plans. A theory of neutrality cannot pass over in silence or
conceal the fact that constitutional democracy has a moral
foundation inasmuch as it clearly opts for the individual and
for equal dignity. Where social and cultural circumstances are
concerned—that is, the opportunities individuals have to express their capabilities—this ideal standard leads democrats (for
example, authors as diverse as Mill or Sen, Rawls or Walzer) to
be presumptively in favor of state intervention. The paradox of
a philosophy of neutrality lies in the fact that it may not disregard real and concrete discrimination and social injustice
without at the same time becoming vacuous. But once it rec-
ognizes the existence of social discrimination, it necessarily
requires the suspension of neutrality or, rather, its delimitation.[41]

The laws ought not to tell us how to love, or if and how
to believe in God. But the question of what the democratic state
should or should not do becomes more problematic and controversial once one has to do with the material and cultural
circumstances of individuals. For example, against economic
liberalism, a democratic vision of politics should lead one to
conclude that the state cannot remain neutral and passive when,
for instance, parents choose not to send their children to school
or when a regional community claims the right to prevent a
minority from practicing its own religious traditions and having a mosque in which to pray. In such circumstances, the
democratic state, in order to be respectful of individual liberty,
must be interventionist, promoting a system of primary education that is at one and the same time compulsory and secular,
and defending religious liberty against those who, in the name
of the religious culture of the majority, claim the privilege to
decide for everyone.

X

Judgment and Disagreement

The citizen has not yet fully grasped the idea that every power is bad if it is not under surveillance, whereas every power is good where a peaceful, clear-sighted, and stubborn resistance is felt.

—*Alain, 1926*

We are now in a better position to clarify the implications of the distinction between egoism and individualism with which we began, a distinction that places in question the relationship between private and public, between morality and politics, in democracy. It was not by chance that Tocqueville had defined the former as a moral "shortcoming" (of the individual), and the latter as a political "shortcoming" of the citizen. Individualism was a political shortcoming because it shifted the focus of interest, transferring it from the public to the private; and since

167

it followed the trajectory of equality, to which it was geneti-
cally linked, it was destined to be reinforced along with democracy and, fatally, to undermine the attention paid by citizens to
politics and to liberty. Democratic individualism was antipolitical, Tocqueville maintained, in the sense that it was a factor
serving to degrade the role of politics, and this in two ways:
either because it turned it into an instrument for the realization
of private interests; or because it subjected it to individual judgment whatever it was, or to the judgment of each, even of those
who were devoid of virtue and competence. Conversely, politics
can be a challenge to individual security and to private interests
because—Tocqueville, like Machiavelli, thought—one does not
readily associate its practice with calm and with individual
convenience, the most important goods for a democratic citizen.
A politics founded upon the sovereignty of ordinary persons,
that is, upon equality, prefigured the transformation of politics,
from being a creative expression of liberty to administration
pure and simple; it signified the advent of a "fatherless" paternalism with which the critics of the welfare state have persis-
tently associated modern democracy.[1] "Nobody is so limited
and superficial as not to realize that political liberty can, if carried to excess, endanger the peace, property, and lives of individuals."[2] But in democratic society the last thing individuals
strive to do is to undermine these goods; nothing is more important here than the guarantee that each take care of himself.
It therefore seemed to Tocqueville that he had to conclude his
reflection upon individualism with a problem rather than a
solution: seeing that a politics tamed by rights, though "human"
and "moral," leaves citizens disinterested in politics itself,
how could a democratic politics be sustained without turning
into a despotism of the political machines flanked by a public
of apathetic conformists? In order to answer Tocqueville's

objections one would have to be able to develop two arguments: first of all, that individualism, rather than obliterating politics, inaugurates a new form of political culture; and, second, that individualism, notwithstanding the fact that it presupposes the undisputed sovereignty of the individual, not only does not disrupt social communication but, on the contrary, facilitates it, precisely through its rootedness in equality and in the politics of rights; that individualism therefore does not nurture a passive adherence but may indeed if anything foster dissent. This concluding chapter is dedicated to the elucidation of these two arguments.

Reverting to the distinction made in chapter 7 between "isolation" and "solitude," one may say, in discussing the first of the two arguments, that the centrality of the private dimension and of moral judgment, so particular a feature of the modern world, can bring about a new form of public action that consists in interpellating politics in the name of the foundations constitutive of democratic civil life, those without which there is no mutual trust, and first and foremost sincerity, a private virtue that nourishes democratic public life because tending to inspire the rule of monitoring, of giving an account to the public. In democracy, political action not only is public but must be rendered public, and brought before the eyes of the public, if the principle of accountability is to prevail. Political action is public in two senses, only the second of which is particular to democracy: because it is dedicated to occupying itself with problems that directly or indirectly concern and affect everyone; and because it must be made explicit, justified, and opened up to the public, always exposed to the judgment of citizens, who in the guise of the sovereign body have two powers, that of authorizing through the vote and that of perpetually judging and monitoring, before or after having voted, those whom they have authorized.[3] It is therefore upon a moral principle—sincerity, which in this circumstance means nonconcealment or explicit revealing—that publicity, one of the pillars of the constitutional state, has its foundation. In *The Future of Democracy*, Bobbio made use of a truly exemplary quotation in order to demonstrate how this idea of the public was born along with the advent of the democratic revolution, namely, an observation by the bishop of Vico, Michele Natale, who in the year of the Neapolitan revolution, 1799, wrote: "Is there nothing secret in Democratic Government? All the activities of those in power must be made known to the Sovereign People, except for some measures of public security, details of which must be divulged once the danger has ceased."[4]

The public nature of political action enables citizens to judge rulers on the basis of two criteria that are, likewise, essentially moral: that of the consistency of political action with the rights and the rules contained in the constitutive pact (this consistency forms the basis of the evaluation of the democracy's keeping of its promises), and that of the consistency of the politician's actions with his electoral promises (this consistency forms the basis of the estimate of accountability or the elected person's accounting to the electorate). The propensity of the constituted power to scoff at this consistency is anticipated and taken into account by the procedures and by political practice—it is no accident, in fact, that constitutions feature norms for the monitoring of constitutionality and the protection of the rights of free expression of opinions, another important strategy of surveillance based upon "making public" what those holding power, even when elected, would prefer to remain private and to be kept secret. It is plain enough that transparency, revelation, and compliance are political categories, and yet they refer to what is the fundamental principle of moral action: individual responsibility, which is as much as to say the transparency of doing (in the case of moral action, the transparency of acting in relation to one's own conscience; in the case of public action, the transparency of acting in relation to the law). The dualism between private action and political action is therefore relative to the rules and the norms, not, however, to the normative foundation, which is common to both areas: respect for others, whether when the actor operates as a private individual or when she operates as an elected citizen.

It is in relation to this moral foundation common to both the public and the private dimension that one can counter Tocqueville's objection that individualism causes politics to wither.

For example, the individual who protests against "corruption" is not an individual who divorces himself from the community but an individual who aspires to a society in which power is not untrammeled and able to elude the surveillance of subjects, and in which those who operate in public are not able to carve out a space of exception with respect to moral and legal norms, are not able, in other words, to disrupt equality of consideration and treatment before the law. Democratic politics marks the end of the politics of the exception rather than the end of politics, because it is the negation of privilege, of justification for violating the principle of equality, and of the argument according to which political liberty is an expression of might. Thus, the second of the two arguments proposed above is likewise confirmed: the revolt against the "corruption" of politics is also a denunciation of the fact that in dishonesty and in passive obedience (which is what dishonesty uses in order to subsist) no real communication is possible between individuals, any more than it is between citizens: "You cannot make an association out of insincere men."[5] This premise provides a structure for the theory of democratic deliberation, and in particular for its three norms: the complete *reversibility* of the perspectives from which the interlocutors produce their arguments (every decision is open to revision); *universality*, understood as the inclusion of all the interests that citizens put up for discussion (no privileges, not even for the majority); and *reciprocity* or equal recognition or respect for requests presented by citizens for public deliberation.[6]

The reference to sincerity (and therefore to trust in themselves and toward others) brings moral custom to the fore. The man in the street, Guido Calogero wrote in 1939, knows perfectly well that it is pointless reminding an interlocutor "about logical noncontradiction, that is, about semantic consistency between what he says and what he has said," if he lacks the will to admit his own inconsistency: "In order to admit the intrinsic inconsistency of one's own discourse, it is necessary, first of all, that one not be in bad faith!" It is therefore not logic that demonstrates morality but morality that renders logic possible, or it is "the honesty and sincerity of the conversation" or, as Kant put it, "good will."[7] "The law is only a memorandum," wrote Emerson. "We are superstitious, and esteem the statute somewhat; so much life as it has in the character of living men is its force."[8] This amounts to saying that the soul of the law is metajuridical and is to be found in the conscience of its citizens. As I explained in the previous chapter, being sympathetic and receptive does not exclude either disagreement or the possibility that each may establish a critical distance with regard to others, as if to wish to guard against confusing a shared acceptance of the democratic foundations with conformism and an unthinking adherence to the most widespread or general opinion as to the best way in which to interpret those foundations. Having a grammar in common, sharing some common goods, does not imply having no reasons to disagree over how and where to apply the rules, or over what to say or believe, over how to interpret the use of these goods. One could claim that suspending action, disengagement, not being too immersed in active political life, even not taking our actual creative and deliberative capacities too seriously, instead of being regarded exclusively as signs of disinterest toward politics should be seen as forms of mental hygiene that each person can practice with herself no less than with others. Socrates had taught his fellow citizens in the Athenian democracy to observe just such a salutary distance, urging them not to accept anything that had not been sieved by their critical reason: the individualism implicit in this message is political precisely because actively engaged in protecting each citizen's sovereignty of judgment.

In a highly instructive book on the culture of rights, George Kateb argued some years ago that a judgment upon political regimes is in actual fact a judgment upon the moral effects that they have upon individuals: we are prepared to tolerate those regimes that allow citizens to cultivate their solitude without that entailing their being deprived of a voice and a political personality.[9] The distinction between isolation and solitude becomes clearer when considered in relation to political regimes. Leviathan is certainly capable of guaranteeing the civil peace and of leaving ample space for private life and for interests, but at the price of exiling individuals from public life, whether in the guise of participation or in that of judgment. Democracy, on the other hand, allows individuals to choose to be nonpolitical without being deprived of the liberty to be able not to be, should they so choose: it does not compel them to be private individuals on a full-time basis, nor, conversely, does it force them to be citizens on a full-time basis.

It is therefore in the relationship between public and private that the character of a political regime is most clearly manifested. Constitutional democracy has the peculiarity of so arranging things that politics, through acting upon individuals *indirectly*, has a positive impact upon their characters and lives. It does not change the potentially corrupt nature of power, but it does change the relationship between politics and morality, so as to enable the former to produce positive effects and the latter to encourage the citizen to attend to the actions of politicians. Where politics is concerned, democratic institutions act as a filter; they lay down rules and procedures that organize collective and individual action, and that act, in other words, upon motivations and upon the will in an indirect fashion. "Modern democracy is, we said, the only regime to indicate the gap between the symbolic and the real by using the notion of a power which no one—no prince and no minority [or majority]—can seize. It has the virtue of relating society to the experience of its institution."[10] The positive effects of the democratic order are manifested first in the nonpolitical sphere and then reflected in the political one, in the form of trust and an appreciation of the institutions, and even of patriotism. From this we can draw a conclusion that may at first sight appear paradoxical: constitutional democracy, precisely on account of its slow, indirect, and unpremeditated educative action, "imparts existential teaching."[11] Contrary to what Tocqueville had supposed, then, it is not so much civil society with its associations and its groups—often far from respectful of the autonomy of judgment of its members—but rather the political system itself, with its representative institutions, rights, and impersonal norms that educates and inspires a dignified moral life in all circumstances involving action, even in ordinary and private ones.

A first important consequence of this normative interpretation of democracy is that in democratic society there is continuous and perpetually open communication between the political moment and the moral, between public and private, rather than a rigid dualism. When the founding fathers of liberalism clarified the distinction between the spheres of life—economic and political, private and public, religious and civil—they presumed that at the basis of this distinction there was a significant sharing on the part of all the members of the community of a code of conduct that prevailed in everyday life and in common sense without its having to be imposed by force. Because only if this condition were met would it have been possible to build a society of autonomous individuals, endowed in other words with a sense of the norm that rendered them capable of acting morally without the presence of a coercive authority placing them under direct surveillance. If to ensure that we abided by the law the sight of a policeman were always necessary, we would have a stiflingly authoritarian society in which none would be free and rights would not prevail. The distinction between public and private therefore does not correspond to a schizophrenic dualism between Dr. Jekyll and Mr. Hyde (a phenomenon that manifests itself if at all when there is corruption or duplicity, two conditions that clearly conflict with sincerity and publicity). Instead it presupposes persons who are capable of assessing the consequences of their actions and who accept the fact that, in some circumstances, as when public figures are involved, private actions cannot help but be in public view because they may have public consequences. Democracy therefore does not render the liberal distinction between public and private obsolete but interprets it without making of the liberal art of drawing distinctions either a sort of Jesuitical justificationism (according to the dictum "the right hand does not know what the left hand is doing") or a hymn to duplicity (democracy represents the end of the *arcana imperii*).

Consequently, the peculiar character of democracy consists in the fact that in it the political order extends the nonpolitical spaces of individual experience. The political virtue that acts invisibly in society is the kind that springs from the idea of right. Thus, it is not only the direct practice of political power that denotes democratic citizenship but also our *knowing how* we may practice politics, and our *feeling ourselves* to be equals in sovereignty, whether we participate directly in it or not. Constitutional democracy is the only regime in which abstract and immaterial forces such as the imagination, ideas, and feelings exercise a real power over things, persons, and relationships. It is no accident that the verbs most often used in Tocqueville's pages on America are "believe," "seem," "imagine," and "feel." The law, which translates into the form of a norm the condition of possibility, perfectly embodies the ideal or transcendental character of democracy: the power of mind over the power of things, the force of speech and of the judgment over physical force and coercion. "By means of the idea of rights men have defined the nature of license and tyranny. Guided by its light, we can each of us be independent without arrogance and obedient without servility. When a man submits to force, that surrender debases him; but when he accepts the recognized right of a fellow mortal to give him orders, there is a sense in which he rises above the giver of commands. No man can be great without virtue, nor any nation great without respect for rights; one might almost say that without it there can be no society, for what is a combination of rational and intelligent beings held together by force alone?"[12]

Democracy returns politics to a radically human dimension, demystifies it, and renders it prosaic and ordinary, in the service of the questions large and small that preoccupy individuals, and of the rights and interests that the ceaseless alteration in material circumstances multiplies and makes specific. Contrary to appearances, then, politics acquires importance not despite but because it ceases to be an art for the few that requires exceptional capacities or that, more radically, comes close to imposing a divorce from morality. Far from marking the end of politics, democracy represents a sort of glorification of it. Two important clarifications are, however, in order here: politics must abide by constitutional rules, and it must be able, as I have said, to act in public and indirectly upon the mind and the actions of citizens; the good that politics produces is manifested outside its sphere, in a "way of living in the world." Democracy's superiority over the other political regimes lies in precisely this capacity to permit escape from politics without politics for its part evading liberty and law. This superiority is expressed in the impersonal character of the rules themselves: it is the enduringly repetitive nature of routine that shapes the habits of mutual respect, that renders natural and mechanical something which, were it to be left to voluntary decision, would remain uncertain and fatally exposed to force and to caprice. Democratic institutions, in other words, permit obedience to laws without creating subaltern statuses and docility, and, at the same time, without prompting citizens to become militant citizens.

If democratic society is not turbulent but always agitated, in Tocqueville's opinion that is due to the fact that its citizens do not have a burning desire to rush to the assemblies, and yet cannot help paying attention to whatever is stirring in the political world, commenting, criticizing, and approving what the politicians are doing and asking of them. The impression one has is that everything is being monitored by everyone, although few concern themselves with such things directly, and that all are interested in politics though they may profess to despise it and do in fact keep their distance from it. The people does not sit permanently in the assembly but follows its proceedings avidly in everyday life, speaking and reasoning "as if" it were always in session there. If Tocqueville found it hard to explain the role of politics in democracy, it was because while on the one hand the clear division between civil society and political society relegated the latter to being an irksome and apparently secondary affair, on the other hand there was no aspect of political life that did not concern society and individuals (everyone was a devout reader of his daily newspaper, Hegel remarked, as once he had been of the Gospel). More particularly, politics seemed to be the only great passion capable of moving Americans, so much so, indeed, that literary and discursive style was modeled upon it. "An American does not know how to converse, but he argues; he does not talk, but expatiates. He always speaks to you as if addressing a meeting."[13]

Might one infer that the need to intervene actively in politics denotes a flaw in a democracy? That the democratic citizen intervenes in politics when politics is the cause of problems? That mistrust is essentially not a sign of crisis in the institutions but rather an indication of their stability? Emerson, for example, said that he had been compelled to engage in politics when slavery had become a threat to the liberty of the entire Union and, above all, to the moral life of Americans. Entering politics was a necessity: the law that obliged citizens of the states in the North to denounce runaway slaves and to have them sent back to their "rightful owners" did not leave one at liberty not to intervene, to stay aloof, to speak "as if" addressing an assembly. They had rather to become "active" citizens and rush to the assemblies. "The last year has forced us all into politics, and made it a paramount duty to seek what it is often a duty to shun. We do not breathe well. There is infamy in the air. . . . I have lived all my life in this State, and never had any experience of personal inconvenience from the laws, until now . . . I find the like sensibility in my neighbors; and in that class who take no interest in the ordinary questions of party politics."[14]

It is against the corruption of those who have been chosen to handle public business that the moral conscience rebels and impels anyone who hearkens to it to engage in active and direct politics in the name of principles: an objective condition of immorality or injustice, a circumstance that should be exceptional and that cries out for a remedy in order that one and all may revert to being free to be, as before, a private or a public individual—as we saw in chapter 4, Machiavelli himself had recognized that what the many desire is to live safely and securely so as to be able to enjoy a liberty that today we would call "negative," in other words, to go about their business and live their everyday life in peace. When it assumes a direct form, participation in politics therefore acquires a defensive and extraordinary character; it is, however, no longer the art of great men, an art that confers divinity and glory upon the few, an art of manipulation and concealment—vices that only a glorious outcome can redeem. In democracy there is no place either for the Aristotelian vision of politics (as an art through which the individual expresses the best of himself) or for the republican one (as a site of duty and of civic identity, of sacrifice), although the relationship with politics is not one of absolute refusal or of instrumentality. "Only in exceptional moments of rapid and profound transformation can political activities absorb all energies and become predominant and exclusive."[15] In "normal" times, active or militant political action veers off toward the horizon, persisting in the form of an interest in what is happening, as Tocqueville said.

The reading of a daily paper, discussion among friends, taking part in the associations that interest us the most are the political phenomena peculiar to democratic life, in conformity with the character of the society and of its individual, entities that are both of them plural, mistrustful of every form of monopoly (even that of politicization) and careful to defend diversified spaces of competences and functions. The fanatical individual, or he who aspires to smooth out this plurality once and for all, who concentrates "all his own energies in only one of the spheres" is without a doubt an individualist, but he is not democratic.[16] Albert Hirschman has proposed a theory of the private-public-private cycle of participation that hinges upon the interpretation of "disillusionment"—or mistrust—as a spur that shifts the quest for satisfaction of needs or of happiness from one area to the other and that confirms Tocqueville's observation and Emerson's opinion. The outcome of Hirschman's theory is that the dichotomous dualism between individual liberty and political liberty—between the liberty of the moderns and that of the ancients—should be replaced by a cyclical approach that accounts for the phases of growth in political interest and those of its decline in terms of the pursuit of happiness, of individual gratification.[17]

The work of citizens in democracies is anything but easy therefore, even if it does not require any specific competence, because they must accept the rule of the majority without renouncing their independent judgment; and because they have no other force to sustain their active citizenship than the virtue of speech and of feelings, the giving voice to "disillusionment" and "mistrust." This is what lies behind the freedom of the press: when the newspapers report a scandal or inform of the possibility that an unjust law is being ratified, they presume that the information will have an impact upon their readers' consciences,

that it will engage their wills and prompt them to take the initiative in rendering public their critical opinion and their mistrust.
Hence, the capacity to disagree while still obeying the law is the
most distinctive virtue of democratic citizenship and the one
that comes closest to the Socratic vocation. It is not the obeying
of the law that is the citizen's virtue, but rather obeying the law
while at the same time expressing potential or open disagreement.
It is not rooted and widespread trust that is a sign of stability—
since it could indeed be a sign of uncritical acceptance and, in
the longer term, of being unconcerned with the fates of the institutions in whose representatives such blind trust is placed—but
rather mistrust, which sustains the sense of monitoring and
critique, a veritable tonic for the institutions.

   One of the very first to grasp, and with a cogency that has
rarely been equaled, this altogether distinctive negative virtue
of the moderns—indeed, to recognize it as a virtue—was John
Stuart Mill, not by chance an admirer and sophisticated con-
noisseur of Athenian civilization. As early as 1859 he very perceptively intuited that the most important and distinctive
virtue of the democracies is the one that manifests itself in free
debate and in criticism, which springs from the autonomy of
judgment and upon which the actual formation of consent
rests. In free societies, political choices receive legitimacy
through the fact that it is possible to give good reasons and to
enable those who obey to reconstruct those reasons by and for
themselves; and finally, to judge them positively or negatively.
If, then, obeying laws approved by the majority is the citizen's
basic political virtue, the exercise of disagreement toward opinions relating to moral and political beliefs and to political
conduct and to the laws is an equally important virtue. Dissent
defends the prerogatives of individual judgment and therefore
protects democratic institutions from the possibility that those

who run them may shut themselves off from society, indulge in abuses, and exercise privileges. Dissent is thus the "civic" force of a liberty that arises in opposition to the pan-civism of the liberty of the ancients, in the name of the moral autonomy of the individual.

Seen from this angle, the distinction between *direct* politics (citizens vote directly on all the laws) and *indirect* politics (citizens elect those who will vote on the laws) can open up interesting lines of interpretation rather than be used to raise barriers between ideal democracy and real democracy. Indeed, this distinction suggests a delimitation of the institutional and sociocultural spaces within which the various elements engaged in democratic political action are expressed—from the formation of opinion in political movements and in the press, to the expression of will in voting, to the decision-making process in institutions, and finally to forms of contestation and monitoring, and, once again, to voting. By having our argument hinge upon a presence manifested through ideas—speaking and listening—we are able to conceive of participation and the institutions not as antithetical but as complementary forms that determine the continuum of democratic political action. Democracy therefore resides in the actual political process that the dialectic between, so to speak, active action and the critical action of checking establishes. To these theoretical premises Pierre Rosanvallon has given the name of negative power or of counterdemocracy, the outcome of a never resolved dialectic between trust and mistrust—a complex and diverse world that the action of judgment sets in motion in a continuous dynamic of reactions of civil society to the actions of government.[18] Instead of concentrating upon what democracy is, Rosanvallon proposes opportunely to study what it is that democracy does in a negative guise, namely, that series of actions which are designed to exert pressure, to criticize, to censure the working of the institutions, or which, in other words, *subvert* the political order from within, peacefully and without destroying it.

Counterpolitics is therefore not to be confused with antipolitics. Counterpolitics designates the distance between institutional politics and a politics that is external to the institutions and serves to impart energy to the former by keeping the latter in motion. We are concerned here with terms that denote the setting in motion of *mistrust* (of disillusionment, according to Hirschman's anticipatory intuition), when this feeling of mistrust, from being no more than a symptom of dissatisfaction, is translated into an active force that engenders forms of counterpower, of open dissent. Counterpolitics is the implementation of the *réserve de défiance* that serves to unmask the usurpation suffered by democracy through the corruption or abuse of representative institutions.

Politics in the guise of dissent and critical monitoring recasts in an original fashion the forms of negative politics produced by the two most important traditions of Western political thought, that is to say, the republican and the liberal. The long and venerable tradition of powers of censorship and resistance, from the Roman institution of the tribunate to the modern checks on constitutionality, is intertwined in the modern period with the reutilization in a liberal key of the revolutionary conception of surveillance (proposed first by James Madison and then by Benjamin Constant with a view to protecting liberty from the inevitable risks that the emptying out of the legitimacy of representative institutions may entail). Opinion that presses government, judgment that vets and censors will—this is the logic that leads us to interpret mistrust not only as an obstacle, as it is in the liberal tradition, but also as active action pure and simple. Indeed, if liberal mistrust manifests itself as "preventative power" implemented by institutions of juridical monitoring or by automatic mechanisms involving checks and balances, democratic mistrust, for its part, sets in motion direct or extrainstitutional actions through which citizens exercise citizenship in its critical form. These expressions of negative politics are different from the liberal ones because they are designed to express disapproval and denunciation of the dysfunctions and abuses of the constituted power *in the name of* democratic promises. Whereas at the origin of the negative action within liberal practices there is an undeniable *mistrust of politics*, at the origin of counterpolitics there is *mistrust of institutionalized politics*. In the former case the aim is essentially to protect the private individual in her rights and interests, whereas in the latter case the aim is to regenerate democracy and to reassert the political rights of the citizen. Vigilance, denunciation, and petition (the three forms of the "powers of surveillance") exert pressure upon democratic institutions in order to denounce the entropy of representativity from which they suffer. The critical action of civil society is an active and constructive expression that confirms trust in politics.

Obviously, this prompts one to think of representation as a democratic institution that sets out not only to legitimize with electoral consent the division of labor between those who hold power and those who exercise it, but also so to arrange things that the election does not absolve the elected from the task of representing the opinion of citizens, even though the citizens do not dispose of any coercive power to compel their representatives to listen to them. Consequently, while it is the vote that lends legitimate authority to the representatives, it is in fact the circulation of judgment between the "inside" and the "outside" of the institutions that imparts representativity to representation. The negative politics of criticism and dissent exerts pressure on the institutions, not from the point of view of the popular will (it is the suffrage that accords this type of legitimacy), but from that of the judgment that the citizens exercise constantly, keeping the institutions under floodlights, so to speak. Negative politics is set in motion not by the people-as-electors but by the people-as-judges, in the indirect forms of dissent, veto, and censure.

Alongside the inescapable criterion of the division of power inherited from the liberal tradition, then, modern democracy avails itself of another important instrument serving as a check: the surveillance of power. We are concerned here with an instrument that arises in civil society and is peculiarly modern; the public expression of a power rooted in the "private" and mental dimension of "judge for yourself." Since democratic legitimacy is based upon consent, upon the autonomy of judgment and upon the mutual respect for ideas, dissent becomes a constitutive virtue. Dissent and sovereignty of judgment are not simplistically cast in an antiauthority role or as a reaction to the power of the majority but also have a role of consolidating self-culture; they are therefore at once a private and a public virtue. Even though they corrode the social sentiments, they reinforce sympathy and cooperation between citizens since, as we all know only too well, we discuss and wax passionate about the things which we love and to which we are bound by ties deeper than rational assent. Finally, they mitigate the tendency to cultural uniformity that is inherent in democratic society and bolster acceptance of majority rule as a method for making decisions that is based upon a recognition of the equal fallibility of citizens, and of their right to review opinions and decisions taken. This richness of political action certainly does not tally with the classical conception of politics; yet nor is it explicable in an economistic vein in terms of calculated efforts to attain an objective and material goal. The fact that it does not fit perfectly with the schemas of the classical politician and of the classical modern—involving glory on the one hand and ascertainable reward on the other—does not mean that it designates the end of politics. Nor, moreover, should we take as norm what was the stance of many liberals, and indeed the starting point of the present book, whereby they considered political participation to be a noble but onerous activity, to be undertaken only by the few, associated with sacrifice and no longer attractive to modern citizens. Hirschman perceptively observed, in endeavoring to correct this commonly held opinion, that it is significant that very often "the citizen's exertions for the public happiness" are compared to "the pleasurable experiences of eating and drinking: we speak of citizens 'hungering' or 'thirsting' for justice."[19] And these efforts, as we have seen, stem from a feeling of dissatisfaction and disillusionment with, or mistrust of, the tenor and quality of public life; a feeling that prompts the individual to pay attention and to seek to check, and that consolidates a salutary habit of judgment and dissent, the habit of a political virtue that is better adapted to a society of individuals.

Notes

Introduction

Epigraph. Benjamin Constant, *Principles of Politics Applicable to All Representative Governments* (1815), in *Political Writings*, translated and edited by Biancamaria Fontana, Cambridge: Cambridge University Press, 1988, p. 182.

1. Brian Barry, *Why Social Justice Matters*, Cambridge: Polity, 2005, p. 236.

2. For Michael Sandel and Alasdair MacIntyre solidarity among citizens is the cement of a communitarian republic, which liberalism erodes because of its individualistic character (Michael Sandel, *Democracy's Discontent: America in Search of a Public Philosophy*, Cambridge, Mass.: Harvard University Press, 1995; Alasdair MacIntyre, *After Virtue: A Study in Moral Theory*, Notre Dame, Ind.: University of Notre Dame Press, 1981). According to Maurizio Viroli, political liberty rests on people's duty toward the community, construed as an ethical, and even religious, sentiment that the liberal exaltation of individual rights serves to debilitate (*Republicanism*, New York: Farrar, Straus, 2002).

3. The question as to whether liberalism can legitimately claim a nonethical foundation (that is to say, be a political order that does not foster individualism) has been at the heart of the discussion between liberals and communitarians in the past three decades; see, in particular, Alasdair McIntyre, *Whose Justice? Which Rationality?* Notre Dame, Ind.: University of Notre Dame Press, 1988, and Michael Sandel, *Liberalism and The Limits of Justice*, Cambridge: Cambridge University Press, 1982. For an overview of the communitarian vision of life see, among others, Robert N. Bellah et al., *Habits of the Heart: Individualism and Commitment in American Life*, Berkeley: University of California Press, 1985 (2nd ed., with a new introduction, 1996),

and Christopher Lasch, *The True and Only Heaven: Progress and Its Critics*, New York: Norton, 1991.

4. Antonio Gramsci, *Individualismo e collettivismo* (1918), in *Opere*, vol. 8, *Scritti giovanili 1914–1918*, Turin: Einaudi, 1958, p. 188. All translations of non-English sources, unless otherwise indicated, are by Martin Thom.

1
Democratic Individualism

Epigraph. Alexis de Tocqueville, *Democracy in America*, edited by J. P. Mayer, translated by George Lawrence, New York: Harper and Row, 1966, p. 14.

1. John Lilburne, *The Free-man's Freedom Vindicated* (1646), in *Puritanism and Liberty: Being the Army Debates (1647–9) from the Clarke Manuscripts with Supplementary Documents*, edited by A. S. P. Woodhouse, London: J. M. Dent and Sons, 1951, p. 317.

2. Norberto Bobbio, *Il futuro della democrazia* (1984), Turin: Einaudi, 1995, p. ix; the passage cited here is not included in the English-language edition (*The Future of Democracy: A Defence of the Rules of the Game*, translated by Roger Griffin and edited and introduced by Richard Bellamy, Cambridge: Polity Press, 1987).

3. Anna Elisabetta Galeotti, *La politica del rispetto: I fondamenti etici della democrazia*, Rome: Laterza, 2010, p. 4.

4. George Kateb, *Human Dignity*, Cambridge, Mass.: Harvard University Press, 2011, preface.

5. On equality, plural and singular, see Giovanni Sartori, *Democrazia: Cosa è*, Milan: Rizzoli, 2000, ch. 10; and, crucially, Norberto Bobbio, *Left and Right: The Significance of a Political Distinction*, translated by Allan Cameron, Cambridge: Polity Press, 1996.

6. Michael Walzer, *Spheres of Justice: A Defense of Pluralism and Equality*, New York: Basic Books, 1983.

7. Georg Simmel, "Über sociale Differenzierung: Sociologische und psychologische Untersuchungen" (1890), in Otthein Rammstedt, ed., *Simmel, Gesamtausgabe*, Frankfurt-on-Main: Suhrkamp, 1989, vol. 2, pp. 109–295, cited in Loredana Sciolla, "L''io' e il 'noi' dell'identità: Individualità e legami sociali nella società moderna," in Luisa Leonini, ed., *Identità e movimenti sociali in una società planetaria: In ricordo di Alberto Melucci*, Milan: Guerini, 2003, pp. 92–107.

8. *Winston S. Churchill: His Complete Speeches, 1897–1963*, edited by Robert Rhodes James, New York: Chelsea House, 1974, p. 7566.

9. Niccolò Machiavelli, *Discourses on Livy*, translated by Julia Conaway Bondanella and Peter Bondanella, bk. 1, ch. 58, Oxford: Oxford University Press, 2008, p. 145.

10. Albert O. Hirschman, *Shifting Involvements: Private Interest and Public Action*, Princeton: Princeton University Press, 1982, pp. 22–23.

11. Thucydides, *The Peloponnesian Wars*, III, 20, translated by Benjamin Jowett, Oxford: Clarendon Press, 1900, 2nd ed., vol. 1, p. 196.

12. Tocqueville, *Democracy in America*, trans. Lawrence, p. 193.

13. Salvatore Veca, *Dell'incertezza: Tre meditazioni filosofiche*, Milan: Feltrinelli, 1997, p. 171.

14. Autonomy has naturally been associated with equality ever since antiquity, when the demand for autonomy emphasized a condition that did not so much concern relations between persons as those between city-states—in classical Greece autonomy was a quality objectively predicated by the other, and not yet a quality "subjectively" claimed by the single individual as an inalienable right. However, even before autonomy was associated with the idea of fundamental human rights, the argument in its favor was construed as one that laid claim to equality of power or equal treatment and could justify an act of resistance against anyone who violated it. Autonomy and democracy together serve to designate the dissociation of power from brute force and its foundation in consent and in norms, or in the judgment and will of the demos; see Martin Ostwald, *Autonomia: Its Genesis and Early History*, Oxford: Oxford University Press, 1982.

15. Nancy Fraser, *Justice Interruptus: Critical Reflections on the "Postsocialist" Condition*, New York: Routledge, 1997.

16. Kateb, *Human Dignity*, p. 30.

2

Private Happiness

Epigraph. John Stuart Mill, "The Subjection of Women" (1869), in *Essays on Equality, Law, and Education*, edited by John M. Robson, in *Collected Works*, vol. 21, Toronto: University of Toronto Press, 1984, p. 295.

1. Émile Durkheim, "Individualism and the Intellectuals" (1898), introduced by Steven Lukes and translated by S. and J. Lukes, *Political Studies* 17, 1969, p. 25.

2. Benjamin Constant, "De la liberté des anciens comparée à celle des modernes" (1819), in *Écrits politiques*, edited by Marcel Gauchet, Paris: Gallimard, 1997, pp. 589–619; "The Liberty of the Ancients Compared with That of the Moderns," in Benjamin Constant, *Political Writings*, edited and

translated by Biancamaria Fontana, Cambridge: Cambridge University Press, 1988, pp. 307–28.

3. Hannah Arendt, "What Is Freedom?" in *Between Past and Future: Eight Exercises in Political Thought* (1961), New York: Penguin, 1993, pp. 143–71.

4. Eugenio Garin, *Science and Civic Life in the Italian Renaissance*, translated by Peter Munz, Garden City, N.Y.: Anchor Books, 1969, in particular pp. 1–20.

5. Quentin Skinner, *The Foundations of Modern Political Thought*, 2 vols., Princeton: Princeton University Press, 1974, vol. 1; Hans Baron, *The Crisis of the Early Italian Renaissance*, 2 vols., Princeton: Princeton University Press, 1955.

6. Jacob Burckhardt, *The Civilization of the Renaissance in Italy*, translated by S. G. C. Middlemore, introduction by Peter Gay, afterword by Hajo Holborn, New York: Modern Library, 1995, p. 100.

7. Montesquieu, *The Spirit of the Laws*, translated and edited by Anne M. Cohler, Basia Carolyn Miller, and Harold Samuel Stone, Cambridge: Cambridge University Press, 1989, bk. 3, ch. 3; bk. 19, ch. 27. See in this regard the excellent analysis by Giuseppe Cambiano, *Polis: Un modello per la cultura europea*, Rome: Laterza, 2007, ch. 6.

8. Burckhardt, *The Civilization of the Renaissance*, p. 108.

3

An "Ism" to Be Used with Caution

Epigraph. Giulio Preti, *Praxis ed empirismo* (1957), Milan: Mondadori, 2007, p. 106.

1. Arthur Lovejoy, *The Great Chain of Being: A Study of the History of an Idea*, Cambridge, Mass.: Harvard University Press, 1936, pp. 5–6.

2. "The Reformation was an emphatic assertion of the individualist element which had been overshadowed by the authority of tradition and of the [ecclesiastical] organisation": Alexander Dunlop Lindsay, entry under "Individualism" in *Encyclopaedia of the Social Sciences*, edited by E. R. A. Seligman and A. Johnson, New York: Macmillan, 1935–37, vol. 7, p. 676. On the foundations of modern democracy in Protestantism see Guido De Ruggiero, *History of European Liberalism* (1925), translated by R. G. Collingwood, Boston: Beacon Press, 1967.

3. Immanuel Kant, *Idea for a Universal History with a Cosmopolitan Purpose* (1784), in *Political Writings*, edited by Hans Reiss, Cambridge: Cambridge University Press, 2nd ed., 1991, p. 44.

4. John Dewey, *The Need of an Industrial Education in an Industrial Democracy*, in *The Middle Works 1899–1924*, vol. 10, *1916–1917*, edited by Jo Ann Boydston, Carbondale: Southern Illinois University Press, 1980, p. 138.

5. John Rawls, *A Theory of Justice*, Cambridge, Mass.: Harvard University Press, 1971, § 43, pp. 280–81.

6. Amartya Sen, "Capability and Well-Being," in Martha Nussbaum and Amartya Sen, eds., *The Quality of Life*, Oxford: Oxford University Press, 1993, pp. 30–66.

7. Amartya Sen, *The Idea of Justice*, Cambridge, Mass.: Belknap Press of Harvard University Press, 2009, pp. 1–27.

8. Ibid., pp. 253–60.

9. Wilhelm von Humboldt, *Ideen zu einem Versuch die Grenzen der Wirksamkeit des Staats zu bestimmen* (1851), English ed., *The Limits of State Action*, edited with an introduction and notes by J. W. Burrow, Cambridge: Cambridge University Press, 1969, ch. 2; John Stuart Mill, *On Liberty* (1859), in *Collected Works of John Stuart Mill*, 33 vols., edited by J. M. Robson, Toronto: University of Toronto Press, 1963–91, vol. 18, pp. 220–23.

10. Plato, *Gorgias*, 482, translated by W. Hamilton, Harmondsworth: Penguin, 1960, p. 76.

11. Ibid., 483a, pp. 77–78.

12. Friedrich Nietzsche, *On the Genealogy of Morals and Ecce Homo*, translated by Walter Kaufmann and R. J. Hollingdale, New York: Vintage Books, 1969, essay 2, § 12.

13. Antonio Gramsci, *L'individuo e la legge* (1918), in *Scritti giovanili 1914–1918*, Turin: Einaudi, 1958, p. 376.

14. For example, the Italian anarchist Francesco Saverio Merlino, who was attracted by the writings of the Austrian marginalists and convinced that hedonistic calculation supplied arguments in favor of "genuine socialism," that is, the libertarian and anarchistic kind; see his *L'individualismo nell'anarchismo* (1893), *Concezione critica del socialismo libertario*, edited by A. Venturini and P. C. Masini, Florence: La Nuova Italia, 1957; and also the collection of essays *La fine del socialismo? Francesco Saverio Merlino e l'anarchia possibile*, edited by G. Landi, Chieti: Centro Studi Libertari Camillo Di Sciullo, 2010.

15. Robert Nozick, *Anarchy, State and Utopia*, New York: Basic Books, 1974, p. 160.

16. Claudio Cesa, *J. G. Fichte e l'idealismo trascendentale*, Bologna: Il Mulino, 1992, p. 192.

17. Nozick, *Anarchy, State and Utopia*, 163.

18. Martha C. Nussbaum, "Beyond the Social Contract: Capabilities and Global Justice," *Oxford Development Studies* 32, no. 1, March 2004, pp. 1–18.

Compare the collection of essays *L'idea di eguaglianza*, edited by Ian Carter, Milan: Feltrinelli, 2001.

19. Amartya K. Sen, "Rational Fools: A Critique of the Behavioural Foundation of Economic Theory," *Philosophy and Public Affairs* 6, no. 4, 1977, pp. 317–44.

20. Sen, *The Idea of Justice*, p. 348.

21. John Stuart Mill, *The Principles of Political Economy* (1852), in *Collected Works*, vol. 2, p. 208.

4
A Brief History of Individualism

Epigraph. Pierre Rosanvallon, "Le mythe du citoyen passif," *Le Monde*, 20–21 June 2004, cited by Steven Lukes, *Individualism: With a New Introduction by the Author*, Colchester: ECPR Press, 2006, p. 2.

1. Alexis de Tocqueville, *Democracy in America*, translated by Henry Reeve, London: Saunders and Otley, 1840, vol. 3, p. 202 note.

2. Alexis de Tocqueville, *Democracy in America*, edited by J. P. Mayer, translated by George Lawrence, New York: Harper and Row, 1966, p. 506.

3. Ibid., p. 429.

4. I take these quotations of Veuillot and the anonymous reviewer from Steven Lukes, *Individualism: With a New Introduction by the Author*, Colchester: ECPR Press, 2006, pp. 24 and 38.

5. Jürgen Habermas, "Religion in the Public Sphere," *European Journal of Philosophy* 14, no. 1, 2006, 1–25.

6. Anna Elisabetta Galeotti, *La politica del rispetto: I fondamenti etici della democrazia*, Rome: Laterza, 2010, p. 4.

7. Thus Koenraad W. Swart, " 'Individualism' in the Mid-Nineteenth Century (1826–1860)," *Journal of the History of Ideas* 23, 1962, p. 78; Joseph de Maistre, *Extrait d'une conversation entre J. de Maistre et M. Ch. de Lavau*, in *Oeuvres Complètes*, Lyons: Vitte et Perrussel, 1884–86, vol. 14, *Correspondance*, vol. 6, *1817–1821*, pp. 284–86.

8. *Doctrine de Saint-Simon. Exposition. Première année, 1829*, Paris: Au Bureau de l'organisateur, 1830 (2nd ed.), pp. 302–3 (where the term "individualism" is used to refer to the theories of Locke, Reid, and Condillac because they held "individual conscience" to be the source of every authority); Auguste Comte, *Discours sur l'ésprit positif*, Paris: Carilian-Goeury et Dalmont, 1844, p. 72. But see also the text by an author much loved by Mazzini, Félicité de Lamennais, *Des Progès de la révolution et de la guerre contre l'église (1829)*, in *Oeuvres complètes*, Paris: Cailleux, 1836–37, vol. 9, pp. 17–18.

Notes to Pages 55–66

193

9. De Maistre, *Extrait d'une conversation*, p. 285.

10. Ibid., p. 286.

11. Joseph de Maistre, *Étude sur la Souveraineté* (written between 1794 and 1796), in *Oeuvres Complètes*, vol. 1, pp. 465–68.

12. Edmund Burke, "Speech on the Economical Reform" (11 February 1780), in *The Writings and Speeches of Edmund Burke*, vol. 3, edited by W. M. Elofson and John A. Woods, Oxford: Clarendon Press, 1996, p. 527.

13. Edmund Burke, *Reflections on the Revolution in France* (1790), London: Penguin Books, 1984, pp. 187, 172, 168, 177.

14. Quoted by Tocqueville in *Democracy in America*, trans. Lawrence, p. 46.

15. Thomas Carlyle, *On Heroes, Hero-Worship, and the Heroic in History* (1840), in *The Norman and Charlotte Strouse Edition of the Writings of Thomas Carlyle*, edited by Michael K. Goldberg, Berkeley: University of California Press, 1993, lecture 4, pp. 99–131.

16. Friedrich A. von Hayek, *Individualism and Economic Order*, Chicago: University of Chicago Press, 1948, pp. 1–32.

17. Friedrich A. von Hayek, *Law, Legislation and Liberty: A New Statement of the Liberal Principles of Justice and Political Economy*, London: Routledge and Kegan Paul, 1973, vol. 1, p. 85.

18. Bernard de Mandeville, *The Fable of the Bees* (1723), edited by Phillip Harth, London: Penguin Books, 1970, p. 201.

19. Adam Smith, *An Inquiry into the Nature and Causes of the Wealth of Nations* (1776), edited by R. H. Campbell and A. S. Skinner, Oxford: Clarendon Press, 1976, vol. 1, pp. 26–27.

20. To obviate the precariousness of the voluntaristic ethics of "deciding to decide," it would be helpful to create "external" supports, or moral habits, as Tocqueville himself supposed; see Jon Elster, *Ulysses and the Sirens: Studies in Rationality and Irrationality*, Cambridge: Cambridge University Press, 1979, p. 43.

21. David Hume, *An Enquiry concerning the Principles of Morals*, section 6, part 1, in *Enquiries concerning Human Understanding and concerning the Principles of Morals* (1777), edited by L. A. Selby-Bigge, Oxford: Clarendon Press, 1975 (3rd ed.), p. 243.

22. Léo Moulin, "On the Evolution of the Meaning of the Word 'Individualism,'" *International Social Science Bulletin* 7, 1955, p. 181.

23. Pierre Leroux, *Trois discours sur la situation actuelle de la Société et de l'Esprit Humaine. Troisième discours. Aux politiques* (1832, originally published in the *Revue Encyclopédique*), in *Oeuvres: 1825–1850*, Paris: Société Typographique, 1850, p. 121.

24. Alasdair MacIntyre, *After Virtue: A Study in Moral Theory*, Notre Dame, Ind.: University of Notre Dame Press, 1984, p. 254. For an excellent attempt to depict contemporary communitarian thought as a part of the counterrevolutionary tradition, see Stephen Holmes, *The Anatomy of Antiliberalism*, Cambridge, Mass.: Harvard University Press, 1993.

25. For a critique of the communitarian strategy of economic liberalism see Christopher Lasch, *The Culture of Narcissism*, New York: Norton, 1979, ch. 10. From the left two kinds of response to economic liberalism have been formulated; on the one hand, a critique in the name of progressivist rationality: as Richard Sennett has written, the "cult of the private" imposed by economic liberalism betrays a deficit of rationality because, by effacing class, it compromises the capacity of social actors to perceive their own interests and to be rational in the manner that economic doctrine would have them be (*The Fall of Public Man*, New York: Knopf, 1977); on the other hand, a critique mounted in the name of the paradigm of the "gift," an ethical-communitarian exchange subverting the rules of commercial exchange, but one that also challenges the statism of redistributive justice. This latter tendency is represented by the critique of modernity as embodied in classical political economy, and takes its inspiration from Marcel Mauss (*Essai sur le don*, 1924) and Georges Bataille (*La part maudite*, 1949). For a sympathetic analysis of the antiliberal implications of communitarianism see Roberto Esposito, *Communitas: The Origin and Destiny of Community*, translated by Timothy Campbell, Stanford: Stanford University Press, 2004.

26. Albert O. Hirschman, *Shifting Involvements: Private Interest and Public Action*, Princeton: Princeton University Press, 2002, pp. 11–24.

5
The Individual against Politics

Epigraph. Friedrich A. von Hayek, *Individualism and Economic Order*, London: Routledge and Kegan Paul, 1949, p. 24.

1. Words of the British journalist Samuel Brittan quoted in Steven Lukes, *Individualism: With a New Introduction by the Author*, Colchester: ECPR Press, 2006, p. 9.

2. For a reconstruction of European social and political history in the postwar period, see Tony Judt, *Postwar: A History of Europe since 1945*, London: Penguin Books, 2005.

3. For a reconstruction of liberalism in the age of British imperialism, see Jennifer Pitts, *A Turn to Empire: The Rise of Imperial Liberalism in Britain and France*, Princeton: Princeton University Press, 2006.

4. I refer once again to the excellent essay by Amartya K. Sen, "Rational Fools: A Critique of the Behavioural Foundation of Economic Theory," *Philosophy and Public Affairs* 6, no. 4, 1977, pp. 317–44; a brief history of the creation and diffusion of the moral precepts that turned the Manchester school of political economy into a new popular religion may be found in Lukes, *Individualism*, pp. 41–45.

5. A review of Spencer's social philosophy, of his relations with French positivism, and, finally, of his theory of the spontaneous equilibrium of interests as a cause of liberty and peace, and above all as promotion of a "pronounced individualism" (as against the positivism of Comte, accused of being a harbinger of nationalism), may be found in the introduction inserted into the American edition of *Social Statics, or, The conditions essential to human happiness specified, and the first of them developed with a notice of the Author*, New York: D. Appleton, 1865, pp. ix–x.

6. Ralph Waldo Emerson, "Self-reliance" (1841), in *The Complete Writings*, New York: Wm. H. Wise, 1929, p. 140. To the "philanthropic school," described as "the humanitarian school carried to perfection," Marx attributed the hypocrisy of those who "by way of easing [their] conscience" sought palliatives for real conflicts: Karl Marx, *The Poverty of Philosophy*, Moscow: Foreign Languages Publishing House, n.d., pp. 139–40.

7. Stephen Holmes, *The Anatomy of Antiliberalism*, Cambridge, Mass.: Harvard University Press, 1993, p. 4; see, in particular, Leonard T. Hobhouse, *Liberalism*, London: Williams and Norgate, 1911. An interesting analysis has been advanced by Wolfgang Palaver, "Schmitt's Critique of Liberalism," *Telos* no. 102, Winter 1995, pp. 43–47, where the ethics of liberalism is examined from the perspective of the "abolition of sacrifice."

8. Charles Sanders Peirce, "Evolutionary Love" (1893), in *Chance, Love, and Logic: Philosophical Essays*, edited and introduced by Morris R. Cohen; with an essay by John Dewey, Lincoln: University of Nebraska Press, 1998, p. 274.

9. Ralph Waldo Emerson, *The Journals and Miscellaneous Notebooks of Ralph Waldo Emerson*, vol. 5, *1835–1838*, edited by Martin M. Sealts Jr., Cambridge, Mass.: Belknap Press of Harvard University Press, 1965, p. 203 (entry for September 23, 1836).

10. Friedrich A. von Hayek, *Individualism and Economic Order*, Chicago: University of Chicago Press, 1948, pp. 1–32; on this theme see Lukes, *Individualism*, pp. 94–101; Anna Elisabetta Galeotti, "Individualism, Social Rules, Tradition: The Case of Friedrich A. Hayek," *Political Theory* 15, no. 2, May 1987, pp. 163–81.

11. Ludwig von Mises, *Bureaucracy*, New Haven: Yale University Press, 1944.

12. Karl Popper, *The Open Society and Its Enemies*, 2 vols., Princeton: Princeton University Press 1963, 4th ed., vol. 2, p. 98.

13. Friedrich A. von Hayek, *The Road to Serfdom*, Chicago: University of Chicago Press, 1944.

14. Isaiah Berlin, "Two Concepts of Liberty" (1958), in *Four Essays on Liberty*, Oxford: Oxford University Press, 1969, p. 148.

15. Ibid., pp. 130–31.

16. In the volume *Individualism: Theories and Methods*, edited by Pierre Birnbaum and Jean Leca, translated by John Gaffney, Oxford: Clarendon Press, 1990, one should see in this regard the essays of Adam Przeworski, "Marxism and Rational Choice," and Jon Elster, "Marxism and Methodological Individualism."

17. Sergio Beraldo, "Fiducia, comportamento strategico, efficienza economica," *Parolechiave* 42, 2009, pp. 74 and 76, where one may find a review of, and bibliography on, experiments relating to strategic behavior.

18. John Locke, *Second Treatise of Government* (1690), ch. 2, §§ 6, 8, 13, in *Locke's Two Treatises of Government*, Cambridge: Cambridge University Press, edited by Peter Laslett, 2nd ed., 1970, pp. 289, 290, 294.

19. Norberto Bobbio, *The Future of Democracy: A Defence of the Rules of the Game* (1984), translated by Roger Griffin, edited by Richard Bellamy, Cambridge: Polity Press, 1987, p. 108.

20. For a critical analysis of the spread of corruption and illegality accompanying the consolidation of the welfare state, see Paolo Flores d'Arcais, *L'individualismo libertario: Percorsi di filosofia morale e politica nell'orizzonte del finito*, Turin: Einaudi, 1994.

21. See Sheldon S. Wolin, *Democracy Incorporated: Managed Democracy and the Specter of Inverted Totalitarianism*, Princeton: Princeton University Press, 2008.

6
Economic Individualism

Epigraph. Cesare Beccaria, *On Crimes and Punishments* (1764), ch. XX, in *On Crimes and Punishments and Other Writings*, edited by Aaron Thomas, translated by Aaron Thomas and Jeremy Parzen, Toronto: University of Toronto Press, 2008, pp. 41–42.

1. See Lelio Basso, *Il Principe senza scettro: Democrazia e sovranità popolare nella Costituzione e nella realtà italiana*, Milan: Feltrinelli, 1958, p. 39.

2. See Pietro Barcellona, *L'individuo sociale*, Genoa: Costa e Nolan, 1996, pp. 52–55; Pietro Costa, *Civitas: Storia della cittadinanza in Europa*, vol. 2. *Le età delle rivoluzioni (1789–1848)*, Rome: Laterza, 2000, ch. 7.

3. Josiah Ober, *Athenian Legacies: Essays on the Politics of Going on Together*, Princeton: Princeton University Press, 2005.

4. Robert Dahl, *A Preface to Democratic Theory*, Chicago: University of Chicago Press, 1956, ch. 1.

5. Norberto Bobbio, *The Future of Democracy: A Defence of the Rules of the Game* (1984), translated by Roger Griffin, edited by Richard Bellamy, Cambridge: Polity Press, 1987, pp. 28–31.

6. Max Weber, "The Meaning of 'Ethical Neutrality' in Sociology and Economics" (1917?), in *Max Weber on the Methodology of Social Sciences*, translated and edited by Edward H. Shils and Henry A. Finch, Glencoe, Ill.: Free Press, 1949, p. 44.

7. Steven Lukes, *Individualism: With a New Introduction by the Author*, Colchester: ECPR Press, 2006, p. 81.

8. Friedrich A. von Hayek, *Individualism and Economic Order*, Chicago: University of Chicago Press, 1948, pp. 24–25.

9. "The will of the community, in a democracy, is always created through a running discussion between majority and minority, through free consideration of arguments for and against a certain regulation of a subject matter. This discussion takes place not only in parliament but also, and foremost, at political meetings, in newspapers, books, and other vehicles of public opinion. A democracy without public opinion is a contradiction in terms. Insofar as public opinion can arise only where intellectual freedom, freedom of speech, and press and religion are guaranteed, democracy coincides with political—though not necessarily economic—liberalism," Hans Kelsen, *General Theory of Law and the State*, translated by Anders Wedberg, Cambridge, Mass.: Harvard University Press, 1949, pp. 287–88.

10. Benjamin Constant, "The Liberty of the Ancients Compared with That of the Moderns" (1819), in *Political Writings*, edited and translated by Biancamaria Fontana, Cambridge: Cambridge University Press, 1988, p. 325.

11. See Luciano Canfora, *La natura del potere*, Rome: Laterza, 2009, pp. 6–7.

12. Constant, "The Liberty of the Ancients," p. 325.

13. Ibid., p. 324.

14. Aristotle, *Politics*, 1257b, translated by T. A. Sinclair, revised and re-presented by Trevor J. Saunders, Harmondsworth: Penguin, 1981, p. 84.

15. Benjamin Constant, "The Spirit of Conquest and Usurpation and Their Relation to European Civilization" (1814), in *Political Writings*, p. 76.

16. Benjamin Constant, "Principles of Politics Applicable to All Representative Governments," in *Political Writings*, p. 217.

17. Honoré de Balzac, *Une Fille d'Eve*, in *Oeuvres complètes d'Honoré de Balzac*, Paris: Club de l'Honnête Homme, 1856, vol. 2, *La Comédie humaine. Etudes de moeurs. Scènes de la vie privée*, pp. 572–73.

18. Plato, *The Republic*, 336b, translated by Francis Macdonald Cornford, Oxford: Clarendon Press, 1948, p. 15.

19. Plato, The *Republic*, 338e–339a, translated by A. D. Lindsay [translation modified], London: J. M. Dent, 1907, p. 17.

7
Apathy and Solitude

Epigraph. Aristotle, *The Politics of Aristotle*, 1313b, translated by Ernest Barker, Oxford: Clarendon Press, 1946, p. 244.

1. Ibid., 1263b, p. 51.

2. Ralph Waldo Emerson, "Society and Solitude" (1870), in *The Complete Writings*, New York: Wm. H. Wise, 1929, p. 624.

3. George Herbert Mead, "The Genesis of the Self and Social Control," *International Journal of Ethics* 35, no. 3, 1925, 262–63.

4. Emerson, "Society and Solitude," p. 624.

5. Henry David Thoreau, *Walden; or, Life in the Woods* (1854), in *The Annotated Walden*, edited by Philip Van Doren Stern, New York: Clarkson N. Potter, 1970, pp. 221–22.

6. Antonio Gramsci, *Lettere dal carcere*, Turin: Einaudi, 1971, pp. 80–81, 92–93. Gramsci's description anticipates Foucault's analysis of the system of depersonalization put into practice in modern total institutions, and more generally in liberal society as a whole, where individuality is replaced "by a sequestered and observed solitude," Michel Foucault, *Surveiller et punir: Naissance de la prison*, Paris: Gallimard, 1975, pp. 202–3.

7. Jeremy Bentham, *Constitutional Code* (1827–30), in *The Works of Jeremy Bentham*, edited by John Bowring, Edinburgh: William Tait, 1843, vol. 9, p. 102.

8. Hannah Arendt, "Organized Guilt and Universal Responsibility," in *The Jew as Pariah: Jewish Identity and Politics in the Modern Age*, edited by Ron H. Feldman, New York: Grove Press, 1978, p. 234.

9. Hannah Arendt, *The Life of the Mind* (1971), New York: Harcourt Brace Jovanovich, 1978, vol. 1, p. 185.

10. Gramsci, *Lettere dal carcere*, p. 138.

11. Alexis de Tocqueville, *Democracy in America*, edited by J. P. Mayer, translated by George Lawrence, New York: Harper and Row, 1966, p. 527.

12. The quotations in this paragraph are all drawn from the chapter "Of Individualism in Democracies," Tocqueville, *Democracy in America*, trans. Lawrence, pp. 506–7.

13. Ibid., p. 589.

14. Ralph Waldo Emerson, *Life and Letters in New England*, in *The Complete Writings*, p. 1043.

15. Olson's thesis regarding the impossibility of collective action is based upon the assumption that collective action be identified with economic action, that is to say, calculated in terms of the sacrifice of participation that an individual is disposed to pay, and in terms of the benefits he hopes to obtain. This thesis, Hirschman has maintained (in his *Shifting Involvements: Private Interest and Public Action*, Princeton: Princeton University Press, 2002), assumes that political or collective action is identical in structure to private economic action, and in the end that it is a source of disturbance or sacrifice. It does not take into account the fact that participation in public life is not a "mere instrument for a goal" but rather an action that contains in itself—through the mere fact of being performed—a source of satisfaction or dissatisfaction, independent of the outcome. It can hardly be said that my participation in public life serves to change society, but it may serve to change my perception of society and hence my attitude toward public life, and, as a consequence, my action may indirectly help to condition my world, my society (that is the logic behind article 4 of the Italian Constitution).

8
Identitarian Community

Epigraph. Ralph Waldo Emerson, *Journals of Ralph Waldo Emerson with Annotations*, edited by Edward Waldo Emerson and Waldo Emerson Forbes, *1841–1844* (entry for October 26, 1842), Boston and New York: Houghton Mifflin, 1911, p. 292.

1. http://www.giovanipadani.leganord.org/index.asp.

2. Robert N. Bellah et al., *Habits of the Heart: Individualism and Commitment in American Life*, new edition with a new introduction, Berkeley: University of California Press, 1996, pp. 102–12.

3. Ota de Leonardis, "Appunti su fiducia e diritto: Tra giustificazione e diritto informale," *Parolechiave* 42, 2009, p. 124.

4. Gunther Teubner, *Diritto policontestuale: Prospettive giuridiche della pluralizzazione dei mondi sociali*, Naples: La città del sole, 1999.

5. De Leonardis, "Appunti su fiducia e diritto," p. 125. One should refer also to Gunther Teubner, "Enterprise Corporatism: New Industrial Policy and the 'Essence' of the Legal Person," *American Journal of Comparative Law* 36, 1988, pp. 130–55.

6. George Herbert Mead, *The Philosophy of the Act*, edited, with an introduction, by Charles W. Morris, Chicago: University of Chicago Press, 1938, p. 222.

7. Anna Elisabetta Galeotti, *La politica del rispetto: I fondamenti etici della democrazia*, Rome: Laterza, 2010, p. 92.

8. A surprisingly astute treatment of this question may be found in a number of old texts by Carlo Antoni on the individual and democracy, gathered by Corrado Ocone in *L'individuo tra natura e storia*, Naples: Flavio Pagano, 1993.

9. Hannah Arendt, "Truth and Politics," in *Between Past and Future: Eight Exercises in Political Thought* (1961), New York: Penguin Books, 1993, p. 241.

10. Alasdair MacIntyre, *After Virtue: A Study in Moral Theory*, Notre Dame, Ind.: University of Notre Dame Press, 1984, p. 142.

11. Tocqueville, *Democracy in America*, trans. Lawrence, p. 508.

9
Regeneration

Epigraph. Piero Calamandrei, "L'avvenire dei diritti di libertà" (1946), in *Costituzione e leggi di Antigone: Scritti e discorsi politici*, introduced by Corrado Stajano, with an essay and edited by Alessandro Galante Garrone, Florence: La Nuova Italia-Sansoni, 1996, pp. 26–27.

1. The critique of individualism is therefore also expressed as a critique of moral relativism and of the identitary poverty of constitutional democracy, as may be seen in the case of the dialogue with Habermas that marked the beginning of the pontificate of Benedict XVI: Jürgen Habermas and Joseph Ratzinger, *The Dialectics of Secularization*, San Francisco: Ignatius Press, 2005.

2. Charles Taylor, *A Secular Age*, Cambridge, Mass.: Harvard University Press, 2007, ch. 8; see also Michael Sandel, *Liberalism and the Limits of Justice*, Cambridge: Cambridge University Press, 1982.

3. "Political and social rights still differ considerably and intrinsically from one individual to another, or rather from one group of individuals to another. . . . This means that the affirmation and recognition of political rights can only acknowledge the differences which justify an unequal treatment,"

Norberto Bobbio, *The Age of Rights*, translated by Allan Cameron, Cambridge: Polity Press, 1996, p. 50.

4. Alexis de Tocqueville, *Democracy in America*, edited by J. P. Mayer, translated by George Lawrence, New York, Harper and Row, 1966, p. 538.

5. Cesare Pavese, "Edgard Lee Masters" (1931), in *La letteratura americana e altri saggi*, with a preface by Italo Calvino, Turin: Einaudi, 1953, p. 56.

6. Calamandrei, "L'avvenire dei diritti di libertà," pp. 26–27.

7. Ralph Waldo Emerson, "Natural History of Intellect," in *The Complete Writings*, New York: Wm. H. Wise, 1929, p. 1259.

8. "I would readily concede that when we speak of 'socio-cultural milieu' we are in effect referring to something extremely vague and intangible. . . . The socio-cultural climate is in a certain sense the sum of intangibles, that is, of the things we cannot really touch or measure," Carlo Maria Cipolla, *Storia economica dell'Europa pre-industriale*, Bologna: Il Mulino, 2002, p. 140. The phrase "atmosphere of liberty" was used by Mill in "On Liberty."

9. Loredana Sciolla, "Fiducia e relazioni politiche," *Parolechiave* 42, 2009, p. 54. On uncertainty as a constitutive condition of trust see the classic study by James S. Coleman, *Foundations of Social Theory*, Cambridge, Mass.: Harvard University Press, 2000.

10. Albert O. Hirschman, *The Passions and the Interests: Political Arguments for Capitalism before Its Triumph* (1977), Princeton: Princeton University Press, 1997, pp. 48–56.

11. Ralph Waldo Emerson, "American Civilization," in *The Complete Writings*, p. 1209.

12. Aristotle, *Politics*, 1281b, translated by T. A. Sinclair, revised and re-presented by Trevor J. Saunders, Harmondsworth: Penguin, 1981, pp. 202–3.

13. A. J. N. de Caritat, Marquis de Condorcet, *Réflexions sur l'esclavage de Nègres* (1781), in *Oeuvres*, facsimile of the Paris 1847–49 edition, 12 vols., edited by M. F. Arago and A. Condorcet-O'Connor, Stuttgart: Friedrich Frommann, 1968, vol. 7, pp. 69 and 77; Condorcet, *L'admission des femmes au droit de cité* (3 July 1790), in *Oeuvres*, vol. 10, pp. 119–30.

14. On the revision in a proceduralist sense of the republican idea of political liberty, and its distancing from virtue, see Quentin Skinner, *Liberty before Liberalism*, Cambridge: Cambridge University Press, 1998, and Philip Pettit, *Republicanism: A Theory of Freedom and Government*, Oxford: Oxford University Press, 1997; for a critique of this proceduralist revision of republican political theory see J. G. A. Pocock, "Virtues, Rights, and Manners: A Model for Historians of Political Thought," *Political Theory* 9, 1981, pp. 353–68.

15. Tocqueville, *Democracy in America*, trans. Lawrence, pp. 525–28. See Gabriel A. Almond and Sidney Verba, *The Civic Culture: Political Attitudes*

and *Democracy in Five Nations*, Princeton: Princeton University Press, 1963, and Robert Putnam, *Making Democracy Work: Civic Traditions in Modern Italy*, Princeton: Princeton University Press, 1993.

16. See Mogens Herman Hansen, "The Ancient Athenian and the Modern Liberal View of Liberty as a Democratic Ideal," in Josiah Ober and Charles Hedrick, eds., *Demokratia: A Conversation on Democracies, Ancient and Modern*, Princeton: Princeton University Press, 1996, pp. 91–104; and Josiah Ober, *The Athenian Revolution: Essays on Ancient Greek Democracy and Political Theory*, Princeton: Princeton University Press, 1996.

17. Pocock, "Virtues, Rights, and Manners."

18. John Dunn, *Democracy: A History*, New York: Atlantic Monthly Press, 2005; Fergus Millar, *The Roman Republican Political Thought*, Hanover, N.H.: University Press of New England and Historical Society of Jerusalem, 2003.

19. Philip Pettit, "Depoliticizing Democracy," *Ratio Juris* 17, March 2004, pp. 52–65; I have discussed and criticized these themes in Urbinati, "Unpolitical Democracy," *Political Theory* 38, 2010, pp. 65–92.

20. Ralph Waldo Emerson, "Aristocracy," in *The Complete Writings*, p. 957.

21. Tocqueville, *Democracy in America*, trans. Lawrence, p. 245.

22. Ralph Waldo Emerson, *Politics* (1844), in *The Complete Writings*, p. 298.

23. Anna Elisabetta Galeotti, *La tolleranza. Una proposta pluralista*, Naples: Liguori, 1994, p. 43.

24. Tocqueville, *Democracy in America*, trans. Lawrence, p. 564.

25. Walt Whitman, "Song of Myself," in *Leaves of Grass, and Other Writings*, edited by Michael Moon, New York: Norton, 2002, p. 42.

26. Tocqueville, *Democracy in America*, trans. Lawrence, p. 564.

27. Gustavo Zagrebelsky, *Contro l'etica della verità*, Rome: Laterza, 2008, p. 135.

28. Salvatore Veca, *Dell'incertezza: Tre meditazioni filosofiche*, Milan: Feltrinelli, 1997, p. 202.

29. Thomas Paine, *Common Sense* (1776), edited by Isaac Kramnick, London: Penguin Books, 1986, p. 78.

30. John Locke, *Essay concerning Toleration: And Other Writings on Law and Politics, 1667–1683*, edited and with an introduction by J. R. Milton and Philip Milton, Oxford: Clarendon Press, 2010.

31. Veca, *Dell'incertezza*, p. 207.

32. Guido Calogero, *Logo e dialogo: Saggio sullo spirito critico e sulla libertà di coscienza*, Milan: Edizioni di Comunità, 1950, p. 124.

33. Ibid., p. 132.

34. Jeremy Waldron, *Liberal Rights: Collected Papers, 1981–1991*, Cambridge: Cambridge University Press, 1993, p. 128.

35. Alan Ryan, *The Philosophy of John Stuart Mill*, Atlantic Highlands, N.J.: Humanities Press International, 1990, pp. 235–55.

36. See, respectively, the first part and the second part of article 3 of the Italian Constitution analyzed in my chapter 6.

37. Ibid., pp. 242–43.

38. Brian Barry, *Political Argument: A Reissue with a New Introduction*, Berkeley: University of California Press, 1990, p. 67.

39. A. J. N. de Caritat, Marquis de Condorcet, *Cinq Mémoires sur l'instruction publique* (1791), Paris: Garnier-Flammarion, 1994, p. 88. For an excellent discussion of the separation between truth and will, knowledge and power, touching upon Condorcet also, see Tzvetan Todorov, *In Defence of the Enlightenment*, translated by Gila Walker, London: Atlantic Books, 2010.

40. Charles Larmore, *Patterns of Moral Complexity*, Cambridge: Cambridge University Press, 1987, pp. 50–54.

41. See George Sher, *Beyond Neutrality: Perfectionism and Politics*, Cambridge: Cambridge University Press, 1997, pp. 20–44.

10
Judgment and Disagreement

Epigraph. Alain, *Le citoyen contre les pouvoirs*, Paris: Éditions du Sagittaire, 1926, p. 150.

1. Christopher Lasch, *The Culture of Narcissism: American Life in an Age of Diminishing Expectations*, New York: Norton, 1979, ch. 10.

2. Alexis de Tocqueville, *Democracy in America*, edited by J. P. Mayer, translated by George Lawrence, New York: Harper and Row, 1966, p. 504. There exists a vast and fascinating secondary literature devoted to what the phrase "equality of conditions" meant to Tocqueville. Alessandro Pizzorno has observed that by equality we should understand not only legal and political but also social and economic equality; indeed, for Tocqueville, equality of conditions takes shape through the equal distribution of inheritances among children, a measure that marks the advent of the democratization of the entire social system because it implies the paying of equal attention to all the individuals, who, with the fragmentation of the family estate, in fact take precedence over the "lineage" or the name; hence the dismembering of the caste communities, the end of social inequality, and the advent of political

equality (Alessandro Pizzorno, "Tocqueville e il paradosso dell'eguaglianza," in Marzio Barbagli and Harvie Ferguson, eds., *La teoria sociologica e lo Stato moderno: Saggi in onore di Gianfranco Poggi*, Bologna: Il Mulino, 2009). Pizzorno's interpretation is borne out by the texts of some nineteenth-century American authors belonging to the Transcendentalist movement, among them Nathaniel Hawthorne, who in *The House of the Seven Gables* has the idealist Holgrave say that for society to accord proper respect to individuals it is necessary to have privately owned houses demolished every fifty years or so in order to give each person the possibility of expressing his own capacities without hiding behind or succumbing to the crushing weight of tradition and family. Taxation of bequests and inheritance was one of the most important themes featuring in nineteenth-century debates about fiscal policies of redistributive justice, and had in Mill a fervent advocate; in the twentieth century the theme was revived by a number of other theorists of democratic society, among them Dewey and Rawls.

3. Norberto Bobbio, *The Future of Democracy: A Defence of the Rules of the Game* (1984), translated by Roger Griffin, edited by Richard Bellamy, Cambridge: Polity Press, 1987, pp. 79–97.

4. Ibid., p. 82.

5. Thomas Carlyle, *On Heroes, Hero-Worship, and the Heroic in History* (1840), in *The Norman and Charlotte Strouse Edition of the Writings of Thomas Carlyle*, Berkeley: University of California Press, 1993, p. 109.

6. Jürgen Habermas, *Moral Consciousness and Communicative Action*, translated by Christian Lenhardt and Shierry Weber Nicholsen, Cambridge, Mass.: MIT Press, 1993, p. 122.

7. Guido Calogero, *La scuola dell'uomo*, Florence: Sansoni, 1939, p. 200.

8. Ralph Waldo Emerson, *Politics* (1844), in *The Complete Writings*, New York: Wm. H. Wise, 1929, p. 297.

9. George Kateb, *The Inner Ocean: Individualism and Democratic Culture*, Ithaca: Cornell University Press, 1992, p. 158.

10. Claude Lefort, "The Permanence of the Theologico-political?" in *Democracy and Political Theory*, translated by David Macey, Minneapolis: University of Minnesota Press, 1988, p. 228.

11. Kateb, *The Inner Ocean*, p. 162.

12. Tocqueville, *Democracy in America*, trans. Lawrence, p. 238.

13. Ibid., p. 243.

14. Ralph Waldo Emerson, *The Fugitive Slave Law. Address to Citizens of Concord, May 3,1851*, in *The Complete Writings*, p. 1148.

15. Bobbio, *The Future of Democracy*, pp. 72–73.

16. Ibid.

17. Albert O. Hirschman, *Shifting Involvements: Private Interest and Public Action*, Princeton: Princeton University Press, 1982, p. 8.

18. Pierre Rosanvallon, *Counter-democracy: Politics in an Age of Distrust*, Cambridge: Cambridge University Press, 2008.

19. Hirschman, *Shifting Involvements*, pp. 90–91.

Index

absolutism, 13
accountability, 169, 170
Alain, 167
alienation, 80, 103, 126
Alighieri, Dante, 143
anarchism, 45, 191n14
anarchy, 28, 29, 53, 118
ancients and moderns, difference
    between, 29, 33–34, 90, 102
anti-individualism, 10
antipolitics, 123, 124, 183
Arendt, Hannah, 30, 33, 67, 118,
    135, 162
Areopagites, 91
aristocracy, 138
Aristotle, 92, 94, 100, 103, 109, 111,
    134
atheism, 156
Athens, democracy in, 21–22, 91,
    117, 162, 173; citizens dissuaded
    from political abstention, 151,
    152; free speech as virtue, 20
atomism, individualism as, 28, 52,
    53, 58, 115, 135
Austrian school, 75

autocracy, 23, 79
autonomy, 21, 26, 80, 130, 143,
    189n14; of judgment, 144, 185;
    moral, 53, 182

Balzac, Honoré de, 102
Bataille, Georges, 194n25
Beccaria, Cesare, 88–89
Bellah, Robert, 127
belonging, 19, 127, 137, 150
Bentham, Jeremy, 79, 112, 113, 116,
    117
Berlin, Isaiah, 22–23, 78–79, 125
Berlusconi, Silvio, 68
Bill of Rights, 8
Bobbio, Norberto, 13, 84, 94, 141,
    170
body politic, 24
Boston Quarterly Review, 53
British Empire, 73
Burckhardt, Jacob, 32, 34
bureaucracy, 44, 68, 76
Burke, Edmund, 57–58, 61, 62,
    64, 67; on civil culture, 86; on
    memory of past generations, 124

Calamandrei, Piero, 140–41, 143
Callicles, 42–43, 133
Calogero, Guido, 157, 172
Calvinism, 62, 73
capitalism, 6, 43, 73, 76, 95, 97
Carlyle, Thomas, 6, 7, 9, 60
Catholicism (Church of Rome),
    55, 60, 156
Cephalus, 103
charity, 73
checks and balances, 92, 184
choice, 39, 68, 70
Christianity, 30, 31, 32–33, 34,
    46, 75
Churchill, Winston, 19, 20
Cicero, Marcus Tullius, 30, 100, 153
citizenship, 66, 81, 128, 129, 180,
    184; disagreement within
    the law and, 181; as founding
    value of democracy, 25; liberal,
    154–55; place in modern life,
    28; republican form of, 148, 150,
    152–53
civilization, 44, 65, 69
civil law, 41, 60, 84, 131, 132–33, 152
civil liberties, 23, 79, 129, 140
civil rights, 8, 15, 48, 83; function
    of, 16; neoliberal interpretation
    of, 66; paradox of culture of
    rights and, 17
civil society, 7, 46, 72, 94, 178, 185;
    judgment and, 182; solitude and,
    122; trust in politics and, 184;
    voluntary exchanges and, 98
class, 77, 80, 106, 137
Cold War, 19, 65, 71
collectivism, 65, 75, 78
communism, 71, 76
Communist Party Manifesto (Marx
    and Engels), 97

communitarianism, 3–4, 5, 17,
    27, 187n3; antipathy toward
    difference, 52; identitarian, 130;
    intolerant, 25; of Movimento
    giovani padani, 125–26;
    "perfectionism" of, 143; rebirth
    in Reagan/Thatcher years, 67;
    as refuge from politics, 113;
    reification of identitarian bonds,
    137
community, 52, 171, 197n9; of
    belonging, 128; gemeinschaft
    (community) versus gesellschaft
    (society), 129; ideal, 125;
    identitarian, 68, 113
Comte, Auguste, 55, 56, 59,
    195n5
Condillac, Étienne Bonnot de,
    192n8
Condorcet, Marquis de, 149–50,
    163–64
conformism, 136, 137, 172
conscience, individual, 55, 68
consensus, 45
consent, 23, 24, 107, 137, 139, 148
consequentialism, 25
conservatism, 61, 67
Constant, Benjamin, 1, 29–30, 32,
    33, 67, 120, 147; on ancients and
    moderns, 118; on liberty and
    economics of exchange, 97–98;
    on money and political opinion,
    99–100; on private liberty, 123;
    on property and money, 98–99;
    surveillance supported by, 183
constitutions, written, 19, 91
corruption, 112, 117, 171, 175, 179;
    counterpolitics against, 183; as
    internal enemy of liberty, 30; of
    political class, 102

credit, banking, 98
culture of the limit, 18

Dahl, Robert, 92
Dante Alighieri, 143
democracy, 5, 54, 79, 182; as
alternative to aristocracy, 138;
in ancient Greece, 91–92, 117;
Churchill on imperfection
of, 19–20; complexity of, 143;
constitutional, 13, 15, 93, 141,
165, 166, 174, 200n1; culture
and will of majority, 10; as
culture of individuality, 26, 34;
democratic revolution, 170;
foundations of, 27; French
Revolution and, 57, 58; "good"
and "bad," 58–59; imperfection
of, 19–21; impossibility of
identitarian democracy, 139;
individualism as defining
feature of, 6; legitimacy of,
23; liberty in relation to,
24; majority with absolute
power, 108; mediocrity in,
119; minimalist conception
of, 24; moral conscience and,
158; myth of tyrannicide
and, 91; obligatory versus
voluntary participation in,
152–53; political autonomy
and, 21; posttotalitarian, 25;
private interests and, 173;
private morality and, 146;
Protestant Reformation
and, 55; as regime without
specific goal, 142; relation
between public and private in,
175–76, 177; representative, 94;
transcendental character of, 176

Democracy in America
(Tocqueville), 10, 50, 53, 121
democratization, 24, 144
depersonalization, 113, 198n6
depoliticization, 8
deregulation, 80
Descartes, René, 51, 57
despotism, 102, 103, 112, 120–21,
124, 168
Dewey, John, 23, 39
differences, 69, 121, 132, 133,
161, 200n3; equality and, 41;
erasure of, 58; of gender
and culture, 16; ideological,
74; respect for, 5; rights
and, 141
Discourses (Leroux), 65
dissent, 20, 23
dogmatism, 87, 96, 136, 148, 158;
critical spirit against, 125; "false"
individualism and, 76; free
trade doctrine and, 95; popular
sovereignty and, 121; toward
beliefs of others, 157
Durkheim, Émile, 29

economics, 94, 95
economy, 34, 48, 144
education, 2, 74, 103, 144, 164
egoism, 28, 50, 63; antisocial, 5;
industrious, 64; militant, 58; as
negative moral sentiment, 1, 2;
post-Napoleonic liberals and,
66; tyrannical ego, 103
egoism, individualism
distinguished from, 67, 109, 118,
119–20, 123, 143; private/public
dichotomy and, 167; tyrannical
ego and, 103
Elster, Jon, 63

Emerson, Ralph Waldo, 42, 72, 75,
   114; on charity, 73; on Fourierist
   communities, 136; on ideal
   community, 125; on the law,
   172; on moral equality, 154; on
   slavery and politics, 178–79; on
   solitude, 115, 121–22
emotions, 38, 159
empathy, 7, 54, 148
Encyclopedists, 57
Engels, Friedrich, 97
England (Britain), 58, 71, 74, 75, 80
Enlightenment, 59, 61, 78, 158
equality, 9, 16, 51, 57, 121, 171; as
   artificial value, 43; autonomy
   identified with, 189n14; of
   citizenship, 18; of conditions,
   34; education for, 144; equality
   before the law, 54, 89; as
   founding value of democracy,
   25, 143; imaginary and, 142; of
   the law, 135; liberty linked with,
   9, 23, 66
ethics, 34, 36, 145
ethnocentric regionalism, 17
Eukrates, 91
Europe/European Union, 28, 34, 55
everyday life, 9, 44, 145, 154, 175, 179
existentialism, 75
expression, freedom of, 112, 170

Fable of the Bees, The (Mandeville),
   62
family, 34, 50, 68, 82, 123, 144; as
   identitary bond, 128; public
   sphere and, 102–3; training of
   citizens and, 145
fascism, 76
federalists, American, 96
Foucault, Michel, 116, 162, 198n6

Fourierist communities, 136
France, 51, 52–53, 57, 65
freedom, 60, 71, 197n9
free rider, 122
French Revolution (1789), 56, 57,
   60, 66
friendship, 30, 50
Future of Democracy, The
   (Bobbio), 170

Galeotti, Anna Elisabetta, 14
gender, 16
Gorgias (Plato), 42, 133
government, 12, 22, 46, 103;
   consensus versus merit and,
   45; consent and, 84; defense
   of rights and liberty by, 82–83;
   democracy as imperfect form
   of, 19–20; democratic society
   and, 44; equality in law and,
   41; executive versus judiciary
   arms of, 85; free, 15, 112; Greek
   democracy and, 91; hidden
   tyranny and, 88; in Italian city-
   states, 32; laissez-faire doctrine
   and, 71–72, 80; legitimacy of,
   13, 24; majority rule and, 26;
   means and ends in relation to,
   23; minimal citizenship and,
   25; obstacles to liberty and, 79;
   "personification of society" and,
   77–78; separation of powers and,
   60–61; subversion of, 94. See also
   state, the
Gramsci, Antonio, 6, 116, 118, 198n6
Greece, classical, 91–92, 189n14
Green, Thomas H., 73, 74

Habermas, Jürgen, 23, 200n1
happiness, private, 29, 32, 34, 39, 118

happiness, public, 29, 30, 32, 186
Harrington, James, 153
Hawthorne, Nathaniel, 204n2
Hayek, Friedrich von, 60, 61, 62, 65; on choices, 70; on individualism vs. collectivism, 71; as minimal state liberal, 84; on "road to serfdom," 78; on "true" and "false" individualisms, 76, 81–82
health care, 2
Hegel, G. W. F., 100, 178
heroism, 147, 154
Hirschman, Albert, 69, 147, 180, 183, 186
history, philosophies of, 76
Hobbes, Thomas, 77, 79, 107
Hobhouse, Leonard T., 73, 74
human community, 9
human flourishing, 90
humanism, 31, 34
humanitarian intervention, international, 54
human rights, 15, 23, 39, 124
Humboldt, Wilhelm von, 41–42
Hume, David, 64, 78, 163–64

identity: belonging and, 138; of citizenship, 128; civic, 179; communitarian, 17, 150; cultural group identity, 69; existential, 19; liberty to switch, 136; loss of, 126, 132; national, 7; political, 4, 90
ideology, 7, 13, 27, 104, 165; as art of winning consent, 107; transformation in, 9
imagination, 176
incentives, 47

individualism, 28, 169; anomic, 68; antipolitical, 86, 89, 103; antisocial, 17, 52, 59; change in meaning of, 65; communitarianism as alternative to, 5; critiques of, 141, 200n1; democratic, 9, 13; depersonalized, 113; dual identity of, 10; ethical community and, 64; families of doctrines within, 38, 46; identitarian, 163; as ideology, 7, 67, 80, 84; "I don't give a damn" maxim and, 1–2, 120; logic of the free rider and, 122–23; modernity and, 34, 51; origin of term, 54–55, 192n8; politically apathetic, 25; as political shortcoming, 167–68; possessive, 87, 163; religious, 147; romantic, 43, 44; social justice and, 74; solidarity and, 137; stigma attached to, 2; struggle against socialism and collectivism, 65; transcendental, 5; "true" and "false," 76, 81–82, 85; in United States of America, 51–52; in Victorian England, 71–72
individualism, democratic, 13, 47, 128, 159; culture of, 134; economic individualism and, 44; French origin of, 62; identitarian reaction to, 131; local identities and, 126–27; transcendental character of, 135
individualism, economic, 44, 45, 90, 119, 147; politics and, 95; "true," 107

individuality, 26, 30, 34, 42, 128;
  affirmation of, 128; culture of,
  46–47; impoverishment of,
  111; individualism opposed to,
  60; negation of, 116; religious
  individualism and, 38; tolerance
  and, 155; transcendental, 144,
  147; uniqueness of, 162
inequalities, 24, 39, 94
institutions, 31, 40, 41, 54, 93, 165,
  181; citizen intervention in
  politics and, 178; as coercive
  agents, 150; in Greco-Roman
  antiquity, 151, 183; "inside" and
  "outside" of, 184–85; protection
  of the individual and, 145–46; of
  republican antiquity, 33
interests, private domain of, 11
intolerance, 25, 27
Iraq war, 86
"isms," 37
isolation, 116, 117, 118, 169
Italy, 1, 17, 61; Constitution of, 89,
  113, 199n15; federalism in, 25;
  Neapolitan revolution (1799),
  170; North–South divide in, 26;
  Renaissance city-states, 31, 32,
  33, 34

Jacobins, 57, 86
Jesus, 74
Jews, 46
judgment, 53, 56, 135, 144, 186;
  dissent and, 181–82; institutions
  and, 184–85; sovereignty of, 138,
  146, 152, 173, 185; tolerance and,
  159
judiciary, supremacy of, 84
justice, 39–40, 45, 103, 129, 141,
  186; limitation upon political

power and, 165; loyalty and, 130;
  Platonic dialogues about, 103–8;
  politics as, 85; redistributive,
  74, 204n2; revenge versus, 134;
  therapeutic vision of, 76

Kant, Immanuel, 27, 38, 59, 99, 172
Kateb, George, 26, 173
Kelsen, Hans, 97
Kymlika, Will, 128

labor, money and, 34
laissez-faire, 71, 80, 81, 94
law, rule of, 132, 134, 145
Leonardis, Ota de, 130
Leroux, Pierre, 65–67, 68
Leviathan (Hobbes), 79
liberalism, 3, 15, 41, 141;
  antipolitical individualism and,
  87; classical, 161; Cold War, 19;
  communitarianism as challenge
  to, 3–4, 187n3; as culture and
  ideology, 165; Hayekian, 67;
  individualism as central element
  in, 39; laissez-faire, 66; "neo-
  idealist," 73; romanticism and,
  46
liberalism, economic, 44, 50,
  61, 69, 75, 194n25; democracy
  on collision course with, 97;
  identitarian communitarianism
  and, 131; state neutrality and, 166
liberty, 6, 8, 42, 56; of association,
  54; as autonomy, 80; civic virtue
  and, 33; as coexistence of public
  and private, 111–12; culture of
  rights and, 19; democracy in
  relation to, 24; equality and, 9,
  23, 66; as expressivity, 159–60;
  government and defense of, 82;

justice and, 85; law as limitation of, 160, 161; negative, 22, 179; obstructions to, 78–79; from politics, 31, 89, 120; power and, 107–8; private, 18, 90, 93, 123; Puritan view of, 59; religious, 54, 166; situated, 129; "unmitigated," 89
Lilburne, John, 13
Locke, John, 54, 82, 83, 134, 156, 192n8
Lovejoy, Arthur, 37–38
Lukes, Steven, 95
Luther, Martin, 38, 55, 60

Machiavelli, Niccolò, 20, 32–33, 62, 92, 168, 179
MacIntyre, Alasdair, 67, 138
Madison, James, 92, 183
Maistre, Joseph de, 54, 55–57, 59, 133
majority, power and opinion of, 8, 26, 108, 125, 141; courage to differ and, 154; democracy redefined in light of, 9
Mandeville, Bernard de, 62, 64, 74
market economy, 10, 34, 71, 76, 96, 97
marriage, 16
Marx, Karl, 66, 72, 97, 99, 106, 195n6
Marxism, 76, 77, 80, 126
Masters, Edgar Lee, 143
Mather, Cotton, 58–59, 60, 62
Mauss, Marcel, 194n25
Mazzini, Giuseppe, 6, 7, 9
Mead, George Herbert, 114
memory, 101, 124, 129, 159
merit, 3, 45
meritocracy, 56

Merlino, Francesco Saverio, 191n14
Mill, John Stuart, 28, 41–42, 158, 161, 181; on limits of wealth, 96; on "old school" capitalists, 97; on private property, 48; social liberalism of, 71; on state intervention, 163, 166
Milton, John, 153
Mises, Ludwig von, 76
mistake-making, 21
modernity, 31, 34, 50, 141
monarchy, 24, 57, 153, 156
money, 7, 34, 74, 98, 99–100. See also wealth
Montesquieu, Baron de, 32–33, 38, 60, 107, 149, 152
moral action, 134, 171
Moulin, Léo, 65, 66
Movimento giovani padani, 125–26, 129

Natale, Michele, 170
nation, 3, 54, 77, 133; corroded by individualism, 53; greatness of, 176; as identitary community, 68; responsibility toward, 25, 72
nature, 43, 83, 86, 98
neoliberalism, 3, 80, 86
neutrality, theory of, 165–66
New England, townships in, 34
New Public Management, 130
Nietzsche, Friedrich, 43
Nozick, Robert, 45, 47
Nussbaum, Martha, 47

oligarchy, 92, 94
Olson, Mancur, 122, 199n15
On Liberty (Mill), 163
original sin, 82
Orwell, George, 116

ostracism, 92
others, indifference to fate of, 1,
    2, 5, 9
ownership, 9, 98, 102, 109, 118, 131

Paine, Thomas, 156
Panopticon, of Bentham, 112, 116
patrimonialism, 123
patriotism, 52, 66, 67, 122, 151
Paul, Saint, 46
paura e la speranza, La [Fear and
    hope] (Tremonti), 68
Pavese, Cesare, 142–43
Peirce, Charles Sanders, 74
Petrarch Francesco, 31
Pettit, Philip, 153
philosophy, 100
Pizzorno, Alessandro, 203–4n2
Plato, 42, 94, 103, 110, 111, 113
pluralism, 42, 111, 156, 159, 163;
    monopoly of power disrupted
    by, 92; procedural neutrality
    and, 165
Polemarchus, 103
political economy, 96
politics, 8, 30, 47, 54, 104;
    abstention from, 73; as coercive
    ordering of the state, 82;
    counterpolitics, 183; degradation
    of, 118, 122; direct and indirect,
    182; as emancipation, 85; end of,
    186; Enlightenment legacy and,
    78; equality and, 68; identitary,
    157; liberty "from," 19, 31, 89, 120;
    as means to acquire security
    and rights, 34; mistrust of
    institutionalized politics, 184;
    morality and, 167, 173; power
    of finance and, 99–100; private
    happiness and, 34; private

interests and, 168; privatization
    of, 110; respect for persons
    and, 145; of rights, 131; virtue
    imposed through coercion, 33
Politics (Aristotle), 92, 103, 109, 110
Politics (Emerson), 154
Polybius, 153
Popper, Karl, 76
popular sovereignty, 120, 121
populism, right-wing, 27
positivism, 55, 56, 195n5
poverty, 40, 74
power, 95, 115, 134; civil law and,
    132–33; freedom to criticize
    holders of, 20; justice and, 105–6;
    limitation upon, 8, 18; passion
    for, 92, 93; personal relations of,
    98; separation of powers, 60–61
predemocratic societies, 137, 138
press, freedom of the, 112, 180
Preti, Giulio, 37
Prince, The (Machiavelli), 62
Principles of Political Economy
    (Mill), 97
Prison Letters (Gramsci), 116
prison system, modern, 112, 113
private sphere, 90, 93, 110, 123
Producteur, Le (Saint-Simonian
    journal), 55
progress, doctrine of, 72
property, 48, 82, 95, 145, 154;
    industrial, 102; in land, 100;
    money and, 98
Protestant ethic, 87
Protestantism, 55, 56
public domain, 112
public good, 7, 16, 62, 67, 100, 102
public opinion, 17, 42, 108, 153,
    197n9
public/private division, 157, 175

public sphere, 25, 36, 54, 162;
    boundaries with private sphere,
    93; bourgeois family compared
    with, 102–3
Puritans, 58–59, 62

race, 13, 43
rationalism, 57
rationality, 63, 84; bureaucratic
    "cold rationality," 68, 76;
    functional, 35, 56; instrumental,
    130; natural, 82, 83
Rawls, John, 39, 41, 89, 166
reason, 34, 58
reciprocity, 144
redistribution, 80, 83
Reeve, Henry, 50
referenda, 15
Reformation, 38, 55, 190n2
religion, 38, 56, 62, 68, 165, 166, 197n9
Republic (Plato), 103, 111
republicanism, 15, 32–33, 66, 67, 150
responsibility, 46, 54, 66, 171
revolution, 56
rights, 6, 8, 19, 48, 133; culture of,
    4, 46, 173; differences and, 141,
    200n3; individualism of, 17;
    metajuridical significance of, 16;
    natural rights, 58, 82; of person
    and property, 154; politics and,
    34; politics of, 52, 131
romanticism, 38, 42–43, 44, 46
Rosanvallon, Pierre, 49, 182
Rosselli, Carlo, 142
Rousseau, Jean-Jacques, 41, 44, 102,
    124, 148–49

Saint-Simonians, 54–55
science (scientific truth), 55, 56,
    76, 164

secession, economic and cultural,
    25
Second Treatise on Government
    (Locke), 82–83
security, human, 48
self-government, 82
self-reliance, American philosophy
    of, 136
Sen, Amartya, 39, 40, 47, 48, 166
Sennett, Richard, 194n25
sexual orientation, 13
slavery, 34, 65, 102, 109, 149
Smiles, Samuel, 72
Smith, Adam, 63, 64, 96
social capital, 145
social contract, 124
social Darwinism, 43, 72, 73
socialism, 65, 66, 68; democratic,
    77; liberalism and, 74;
    libertarian, 45, 191n14
social justice, 3, 25, 68, 74, 77; "true"
    individualism as negation of, 82;
    undermined by neoliberalism,
    80
society, 53, 71, 144; associative
    forms of, 127; gemeinschaft
    (community) versus gesellschaft
    (society), 129; "great" society,
    130–31; personification of, 77;
    presumed scientific laws of, 76;
    solitude and, 114; "trickle-down"
    ideology and, 2; trust as cement
    of, 63
sociology, 30
Socrates, 42, 74, 103, 105–8, 162, 173
solidarity, 4, 7, 59, 63;
    communitarian, 68; subversion
    and regeneration of, 137;
    superseded by "trickle-down
    effect," 81

solitude, 114, 115, 116, 117–18, 169
sovereignty, 55, 81, 119, 168; of individual judgment, 138, 146, 152; of judgment, 173; popular sovereignty, 56, 121; power of sovereign will, 93; republican idea of, 66
speech, freedom of, 20, 112
"Speech on the Economical Reform" (Burke), 57
Spencer, Herbert, 71, 72, 73, 75, 84, 195n5
spheres of life, 18, 148, 175
Spinoza, Baruch, 156
Spirit of Conquest and Usurpation, The (Constant), 101–2
Spirit of the Laws, The (Montesquieu), 32
state, the, 31, 34, 48, 130, 149; bureaucratic, 68; citizen's dealings with, 67; coercive power of, 98; free market and, 96; meaning of "public" and, 161, 162; minimal state liberals, 84; politics and, 82; reaction of civil society against, 72; role in modern democracy, 69; social functions of, 45; sphere of interpretation and, 165. See also government
statism, 65, 76
suffrage, right to, 5
surveillance, 115, 116, 136, 170, 175; as check on power, 185; forms of the "powers of surveillance," 184; revolutionary conception of, 183

taxation, 2, 81, 83, 122–23, 147, 204n2
Taylor, Charles, 128, 141

Teubner, Gunther, 130
Theory of Justice, A (Rawls), 39
Thoreau, Henry, 42, 115
Thrasymachus, 103–8
Thucydides, 21
Tocqueville, Alexis de, 10, 11, 29, 34, 51, 56; American journey of, 128; on apolitical individualism, 168; on associative forms of society, 127; on communitarian relationships as refuge from politics, 113; on democracy as alternative to aristocracy, 138, 154; on democratic empathy, 155; on egoism and individualism, 67, 103, 109, 118, 123, 167; on elusiveness of equality, 142; Emerson and, 121; "equality of conditions" and, 203n2; fear of democratic despotism, 112; on government authority, 12; Maistre compared to, 55, 57; on newness of individualism, 49, 50; objections to individualism, 167, 168–69, 171; on political action in "normal times," 179; on Reformation and democracy, 55; on religious liberty, 54; on role of politics in democracy, 178; on self-interest, 151; words used to describe American life, 176
tolerance, 18, 155–57, 158; limit of, 165; majority opinion and, 161; as negative attitude, 160; religion and, 54
totalitarianism, 13, 24, 75, 87, 110
transcendentalism, 53, 115, 143–44, 204n2
Tremonti, Giulio, 68
"trickle-down" effect, 2, 81

trust, 63, 146–47, 150, 169
tyranny, 12, 32, 33; alienation and, 109; in modern democracies, 91; monarchical, 24; of public opinion, 42; as system of arbitrary power, 94; tyrant individual in Platonic dialogues, 103–4; wealth and, 88

United States of America, 51, 75; Constitution of, 8; federalists in, 96; founding fathers of, 62; Fourierist communities in, 136; neoliberalism in, 80
universalism, 16, 27
universality, 46, 133, 141, 172
utilitarianism, 117
utopias, 75, 106; antipolitical, 81; of free market, 86; Platonic, 111; pragmatic, 89

Veuillot, Louis, 52–53
Victoria, Queen, 71

Viroli, Maurizio, 187n2
virtue, civic, 33, 62
voting, 15, 122–23, 147, 164, 169–70, 182

Walzer, Michael, 18, 166
war, 30, 132
wealth, 33, 69, 100; charity and, 73; limits of, 96; opportunities and, 39; redistribution of, 83; "trickle-down" effect and, 81; tyranny and, 88; unequal material wealth, 26. See also money
Wealth of Nations, The (Smith), 63
Weber, Max, 26–27, 147
welfare state, 2, 68, 168
Whitman, Walt, 115, 155, 158
Wolin, Sheldon, 87
women, 103, 138, 145, 149
World War, Second, 13

Zagrebelsky, Gustavo, 155–56